HOW TO CREATE

LITTLE
HAPPY
LEARNERS

HOW TO CREATE

LITTLE HAPPY LEARNERS

60 SIMPLE LEARNING and CRAFT ACTIVITIES for 0–5 year olds

Sophie David

Ted, Finn and Edie.
This book is ours – you helped
me to write this from start
to finish. Without you, it truly
wouldn't have been possible.
Mummy loves you.

CONTENTS

INTRODUCTION

LITTLE HAPPY LEARNERS launched in 2019 in a small house just outside London in the UK. When I say launched, I mean I set up the first activity and photographed it for Instagram. That activity was captioned, 'Keeping life PEASful', but truthfully, life was anything but peaceful at that point.

I had two little boys under 2 vying for my attention, and I constantly felt like I wasn't doing enough, that I wasn't giving them the time they both needed and deserved. There was so much to juggle – housework, feeding, cooking, baby clubs – but somehow it never really felt like I was getting much done. I felt like a hamster on a wheel, the days were monotonous and I knew something needed to change.

There was so much to juggle – housework, feeding, cooking, baby clubs – but somehow it never really felt like I was getting much done.

During a feed, one cold night, I was sitting in the dark reading an article on my phone about routines for babies and toddlers. I knew my routine needed to be adjusted, but the article was advocating that children should fit around their parents' routine, rather than parents fitting around their children's. It made me feel very conflicted, but it also got me thinking.

That very night I planned out two play activities, one for each of the boys. I decided that they both deserved some quality time with me and a bit of one-to-one attention every day, and I believed it would alleviate some of the anxieties I was feeling too.

Casting my mind back to when I was a teacher, I remembered what worked best – a play-based environment focusing on the children's interests. I started to think about how I could bring some of that structure and play into my home, and I'm so glad I did.

After making that first post on Instagram, I quickly realised there were lots of other parents, carers and educators out there all looking for fun and engaging ways to get their little ones learning. The feedback I have received over the last few years has been really positive. My ideas are educational, sustainable and often easy to set up, and the enthusiasm I have received has certainly been instrumental in the development of this book.

What does it mean to be a little happy learner?

As a parent and teacher, my main aim has always been to ensure that children LOVE to learn. Once I started to plan one-to-one activities for my own children every day, I found myself thinking about the learning opportunities within each one. I loved knowing that they were learning through play, and it filled me with joy to know that I was nurturing a love of learning in them.

I truly believe that if a child loves to learn, they will always achieve big things. But how do you teach a love of learning? The answer to that is really simple. You have to love it too, and I hope this book will inspire you to try.

About me

I'm Sophie, a stay-at-home mum of three children currently all under the age of 5.

Before becoming a parent, I was a super-organised (verging on obsessive) primary-school teacher. I taught predominantly in early years and absolutely loved my job. From an early age, I had watched my older sister drawing and always wished I could be as creative as her. Stepping into the classroom allowed me to do just that – I was able to indulge my creative self and I've never looked back. I now find a huge amount of solace in drawing and crafting.

After having my first son, Ted, I knew pretty quickly that I was needed at home. Ted was, and still is, a hugger. He loves to be around me, and in those early days he didn't really like being around anyone else. However, before even making the decision to become a stay-at-home mum, I became pregnant again with Finley. I then had two boys vying for my attention, and although it hasn't always been easy, I can honestly say that the decision to stay at home with them was the best I ever made. Since then, we have added Eden to the clan, and she has completed our family in a way we never knew possible.

Despite having always loved the idea of being at home with my children, I found the transition harder than expected. I certainly felt a slight loss of identity as I struggled to find a new balance, and I experienced feelings of guilt, doubt, anxiety and uncertainty. I've since learnt to accept that not every day is going to be a huge success, and some days will be tougher than others. All any of us can do is try our best.

One key thing I've learnt is that planning activities that focus my whole attention on one child at a time is beneficial for all of us. Those one-to-one periods give me a new perspective and help me to feel more connected to each of them.

Rethinking my approach to play and building craft into it has changed life for everyone. I went from feeling that I could never get this whole parenting game right, to feeling a lot more confident in myself. Also, knowing that crafts were being put to good use by the kids was, and still is, a huge benefit.

ARTY-CRAFTY?

As far as the activities in this book are concerned, it doesn't matter at all if you don't think of yourself as a creative or artistic person. Your child certainly won't mind wonky drawings. In their eyes you are the best artist in the world.

Choose a really simple project to start with, such as the bottle-cap ladybirds in Bug Count (see page 50), and your children's response will most probably give you a new-found confidence in your artistic ability. You may even discover some of the benefits of working with your hands and getting outside your head.

When I started this journey, I could not draw and had never been particularly artistic, but I always loved to craft. I promise you that absolutely anyone can craft, and I'll show you how.

Family life

Every family is unique, but the children within them all clamour for the same thing. What they most want and need from us is time, and this is true whatever your work or financial circumstances. Giving children just 15 minutes of our undivided attention makes for a very special connection, and brings great benefits. Why not try making bath time into an activity by adding some plastic bricks or cups to the bath? This is a complete GAME CHANGER, and you won't believe how much talk you get from the children!

What if an activity doesn't go to plan? Either pack it up for another time, or go with what your children are doing.

It isn't necessary to play elaborate games. The key thing is to play to your strengths. For example, I'm not very good at 'playing' in the loosest sense of the term. If I sit down with the kids and play with their toys, I always end up sorting them into groups, which I recognise isn't much fun. My husband, Adam, on the other hand, is brilliant at playing. He is basically a big kid at heart and can play with the children for hours.

The point is that between the two of us we make things work. I plan structured adult-led and child-led play (I'll explain these in more detail later), while Adam enjoys all the independent unstructured play. Sometimes we cross over, but generally we play to our strengths so that we can get the most from our children, and they can get the best out of us.

Take a look at your family dynamics and think about what you're all best at.

Monday–Friday

The daily schedule is different in every family, so let me tell you about mine without being in any way prescriptive. I plan one activity for each of the kids every day. This might sound a lot, especially if you're working too, so plan whatever you feel is achievable for you and your family. Just remember, it doesn't always have to be a grand activity. It can be a simple 10-minute drawing session before teatime. The key thing is that this is completely their time and takes just 10 minutes out of your day.

Every day is different. Some days we complete a few activities, other days we will do just one, and sometimes we do none at all because we're meeting friends or doing other things. Some days, the boys crave one-to-one attention, and other days they are inseparable and want to craft together. I am completely guided by them and their moods.

One activity for each child every day? How do I plan them all?

This is where I tap into my 10 years' teaching experience, because I like to plan a week around a topic or theme. Every Sunday, I have a chat with the boys and give them a few options. I'll say, for example, 'What would you like to do next week? Would you like to learn all about sea creatures or about space?' This may spark a huge discussion, or just a one-word answer, but we always decide together.

I then make a list of as many ideas as I can come up with on the chosen topic. While I can draw on my experience, I also use Instagram and Pinterest for inspiration. I always make sure I have a range of activities, focusing on all kinds of learning, and often end up with a list of around 20 ideas. (I never complete them all.)

Some activities, such as cardboard crafts, require preparation. I gather resources for my favourite ideas and spend my evenings and Sunday mornings (Crafty Sunday) creating and preparing for the week ahead.

Then, day to day, I give the children a choice. 'Would you like to practise cutting or do some painting this morning?' I always try to be realistic about what we can achieve in a day, depending on what other plans we have. By having a large bank of ideas, I can always give the kids ownership. They get to choose, which means they will be more invested in the task.

Weekends

At weekends, we focus mainly on developing the children's independence. We bake, cook and prepare meals together. We prompt them to play together, making up their own games, role playing, completing puzzles and playing board games. Anytime you can give your child space to be entertained and engaged without an adult's support is absolutely brilliant. Children need time to play alone, and even to learn how to be bored. Also, keeping themselves entertained allows you to step away for a while, if only to prepare a meal or empty the dishwasher.

On Crafty Sunday, which we have every weekend, we spend the morning all crafting together, listening to music and eating pancakes. I often spend the time preparing for the week ahead, as I mentioned earlier. We paint, cut, sculpt and stick, all completely immersed in creativity. The kids love it because they get a sneak peek at what is to come, but they also enjoy the togetherness. The kitchen table on Sunday morning is one of my happy places.

Our play space

We are not lucky enough to have a dedicated playroom, so everything we do is done within our living space. Despite that, I like to think the house is still presentable, though you can definitely tell that children live here and are at the heart of our home.

We have different spaces around the house to make play and learning more accessible. For example, a book box is readily available for the children to dip into at any time.

Our sensory table (see page 177) is used daily, not only for its sensory purpose, but for mealtimes and all other activities. Its low height, and the low chairs around it, mean that the children can use it easily.

All our toys are categorised in different boxes: farm, sea, safari, cars, instruments, imaginary play (e.g. doctors, hairdressers), Duplo, puzzles, dinosaurs, etc. We play with one box at a time because it is too easy for toys to become invisible when they are all played with continuously.

In our garden we have a mud kitchen (see page 177), which is genuinely one of our favourite resources. We bought it for Ted's second birthday and it has been loved through all the seasons since. Outdoor play teaches children to manage their own risks while immersing themselves in their environment, and mud kitchens are a brilliant resource for encouraging creative thinking and exploration of nature. Our mud kitchen always reminds me of my own childhood with my four sisters.

Our craft cupboard, where I keep most of our resources, is my pride and joy. It has individual labelled boxes containing a wide range of craft materials; everything from pom-poms and lolly (popsicle) sticks to shells and acorns. At the risk of sounding dramatic, organising this cupboard has completely changed my life. Let me explain.

I can grab a box labelled phonics, for example, and have a phonics activity set up within 5 minutes because everything I need is there. It's perfect! Of course, it does mean giving up a larder or understairs storage space, which your partner might not be willing to do, but I urge you to use your powers of persuasion. Getting everything super-organised in a craft cupboard will make life so much easier. (You can find a list of suggested resources on page 176.)

While I'm a big fan of crafting, I'm aware that one of the reasons lots of parents and carers avoid arts, crafts and messy play is because of the

TIP FOR LESS-MESSY PLAY

*Here's a tip that will CHANGE
YOUR LIFE. For messy play
activities, such as those involving
rice, beans, water beads and so
on, invest in a fitted sheet. Simply
hook it around your table legs or
a few chair legs to trap the mess
and it allows for a much easier
tidy-up.*

MESS. That's such a shame, because messy play can't really be avoided where children are concerned. The best way to overcome this aversion is to mentally prepare yourself that it's going to happen and to have some tools up your sleeve to help you manage the mess.

Taking steps to prepare yourself for mess will allow you to enjoy the activities more, and perhaps even come to love them. Those good feelings will in turn be passed on to your children, instilling them with a love of learning.

My four key principles to play

When introducing a play-based lifestyle, I believe there are four keys to ensure it is effective and brings the most happiness.

PLAN Begin by planning an activity into your day. Write a list of small, achievable activities that you can complete with your child in a week, e.g. play hairdressers, bake cookies, build a tower, cook dinner together, paint a rainbow.

TIME Find a 10-minute window to be with your child and ensure that nothing interrupts it. Let the laundry wait, set aside all devices and play together. Children love to see us playing.

PREPARE Get yourself ready physically or mentally for your chosen activity. Whether it is gathering resources, setting out ingredients or just taking a deep breath, make sure you're in the right frame of mind so that everyone has fun.

REWARD Who doesn't love to see their little one learning something new? That's your reward. The reward for them is having your time, a fun activity and some new knowledge. What else could they need?

Different types of play

Within this book there is a range of different activities with different styles of play. Here are those different play styles explained in more detail.

ADULT-LED PLAY is set up and created with a desired outcome, and usually has a learning intention. The activity is completed by adult and child together. Where that adult is someone other than a parent, children can begin to build relationships outside the immediate family, which is hugely important. Both my boys love adult-led activities, and they always lead to a huge amount of self-pride. They encourage cooperation and build on their listening and attention skills, which are all crucial in life.

MESSY PLAY is a type of adult-led play that is all about creating a controlled mess. The mess is designed to foster curiosity and imagination while encouraging exploration of different textures and the feelings they provoke. Delving around in the mess is also hugely beneficial to children's motor skills; helping to build up the muscles in their hands and fingers. Providing opportunities for children to immerse themselves in messy play is a great way of developing their communication skills, and they also learn to handle boundaries and rules, such as not throwing the mess around.

TIPS FOR LESS-MESSY BAKING

- Pre-weigh all ingredients and put them in separate bowls.
- Have all utensils to hand.
- Use a large ceramic bowl; it's too heavy for children to move around, so will lead to fewer spillages.
- Fill a sink or washing-up bowl with soapy water so it's ready for washing hands and utensils.

CHILD-LED PLAY is set up by an adult, but thereafter is completely led by the child's imagination. It provides them with ownership of their learning, allowing them to take control and show their creativity. This type of play often taps into a child's ability to solve problems and helps to build resilience when approaching a new task. Using building blocks, for example, may start out with a declared aim – 'I'm going to build a farm' – but nearly always ends up taking a completely different direction. Children have a much better imagination than we do.

Remember, you can always involve your child in setting up and clearing away. Many hands make light work, and doing it together is a lovely way of connecting.

FREE PLAY is completely unstructured and independent play. There is no adult input and children have the freedom to explore in any way they wish. My little ones, for example, love to create set-ups, such as an animal kingdom or a town. Such activities provide children with opportunities to question the world around them, and to express their opinions and emotions more freely. My kids also love to role play, and often act out being a parent and baby. Without doubt, they mimic language and behaviours they have witnessed, and this alone can teach you more about your child than any other learning activity.

HOW TO USE THIS BOOK

There are 60 fun activities in this book for you and your children to enjoy. Learning through play is at the heart of every single one, and each has been designed to provide the most amount of fun for you and your child! They have all been tried and tested by my lovely brood, and I can honestly say we have loved them all. I really hope you do too.

The activities are grouped in themes, 12 in all, because this way of working sparks more creativity from me and more engagement from the kids. I also find that a diverse range of topics broadens their learning and helps to develop their knowledge and understanding of the world.

While some themes are best tackled at home, many encourage learning when out and about. For example, you can go on a rainbow colour hunt while out on a walk, or see what vehicles can be spotted while out in the car. Each theme is easily accessible and transferable.

Within each theme are five activities, which can be spread out in any way you want. You could perhaps do one a day, or just one a week – whatever works for you and your family.

The types of play and learning explored in the activities are indicated by symbols (see following page). These allow you to see at a glance what's suitable for your child.

Don't be afraid to change tack. Sometimes children have better ideas than we do.

Many of the activities start with a story element, which is designed to 'hook' your children into that activity. Relating a tale about a fictional character will open up their imagination and create a world of opportunities in your play. It can spark ideas, develop their curiosity and get them asking and answering questions.

Within each activity you will find a list of everything you need, plus numbered steps telling you how to prepare and play.

Every activity has been tailored to suit children aged 1–5, and some are suitable even for young babies. In every case, I explain how you can adapt the activity to a particular age. Of course, children develop at different speeds, so be guided by what you know your child can manage rather than their actual age.

SYMBOLS USED IN THE ACTIVITIES

Look out for the following symbols to see the focus of each activity at a glance.

Adult-led

Problem-solving

Messy play

Child-led

Maths

Phonics

Baby play

Independence

Communication

Creativity

Motor skills

Remember, you can come back to each activity year on year and ultimately complete all the different tasks for each age range. In this way you can observe your child's development, which comes on in leaps and bounds during the early years. This can get rather overlooked in our fast-paced, ultra-busy lives, so take my advice and get a folder to hold all the crafts you complete from this book. You can then go back and see what you have both learnt. It's a keepsake worth keeping.

Here are the FIVE main learning areas that are covered in all the activities.

MOTOR SKILLS Providing opportunities for children to develop their gross motor skills (movements involving large muscles, as in the arms and legs), and fine motor skills (movements involving small muscles, such as those in the hands and wrists). The latter can begin from the age of 6 months, by encouraging your baby to use the pincer grip (thumb and index finger) to pick up small objects. By the time they are 2 years old, your child can begin to practise using scissors.

PROBLEM-SOLVING Providing opportunities for children to connect previous knowledge with new learning. This takes the form of mathematical, scientific, reading and writing activities. For example, by 18 months your child can be sorting objects into groups, and by the age of 3 can be counting chronologically.

COMMUNICATION Providing opportunities for children to develop their speaking and listening skills, to convey their feelings, and to share new ideas. At 6 months, for example, they are expressing their needs with simple cries and squeals, and by 4 years old they are articulating their needs and wishes. Each communication activity includes some key vocabulary for each age range.

CREATIVITY Providing opportunities for self-expression to encourage children to create, perform and use their imagination freely. It includes arts and crafts, musical experiences and role playing. At 6 months, for example, a child is experimenting with sound and movements, and by 5 years is expressing imagination, feelings and creativity through art and music.

INDEPENDENCE Providing opportunities for children to try out new skills and build confidence in completing them with little or no adult support. At 12 months, for example, a child can be using a spoon for eating, and by 3 years can be able to cut up the food on their plate.

Phonics

Entwined in the activities throughout this book you will find lots of links to phonics.

Phonics is a way of teaching children to read and write, and it's more straightforward than the jargon surrounding it might suggest. In the English language there are 26 letters and 44 sounds. Each sound can be written as a single letter or a combination of letters, and we combine those sounds to make words.

As soon as your child starts their journey in education, they will begin to learn phonics, so some simple activities will set them up with the confidence they need to thrive. You could start at bath time by putting some foam letters in the bath. We play a game where the boys stick the letters to their bodies and we make the sounds together. It becomes a fun activity rather than a lesson.

One question that seems to be on every parent's mind when it comes to phonics concerns lower case and capital letters. Which should you teach first? The answer to that is teach them both! I usually show the capital and lower case letter together and tell the children the letter name and sound. Take S, for instance: I say 'Ess' is the letter name, and 'sssss' is the sound it makes.

When should you start teaching phonics? There is no right answer. My eldest son, Ted, wanted to learn about letters and sounds from the age of 2, but his brother, Finn, was nearly 3 before he started showing an interest. My advice is to be guided by your children. They will begin to show signs that they are ready by asking what words say, pointing to shop signs and noticing their name. When they begin to show interest, grab the opportunity with both hands.

Phonics may seem complicated and perhaps a bit confusing, but with the activities in this book, you will be teaching your child phonics without even knowing it!

Early maths

The best way for your children to learn maths is through play, using simple games that generate no fear of getting things 'wrong'.

Many of the tasks in this book do exactly that, incorporating problem-solving and number work, but in the easiest ways possible. For example, by adding a simple counting opportunity into an activity, you will begin to show your children that all objects can be counted, and they will naturally begin to do this in their own independent play. By encouraging your children to use mathematical language in these play-based activities, you are building a knowledge that they can use confidently.

Upon beginning school, children will be involved in daily maths-based activities, so teaching some early maths skills before they start will help to develop a curiosity and confidence surrounding numbers. I can honestly say there is never a right time to begin counting and noticing shapes in your environment. I began counting with my little ones as soon as they could sit up and grasp objects. I would help them to count their cars and animals, the steps we climbed, the toys we put in the bath... the opportunities were endless – and fun!

Age groups and typical milestones

Milestones are physical and behavioural developments that occur during childhood, and children may meet them at different ages. My mantra is always 'a parent knows their child best', so gauge the milestones by what you know of your child and their abilities. My three little ones were all premature and developed at completely different rates, so rarely fitted within the age range they belonged to. However, if you are concerned about your child's development, always check with a health-care professional.

In order to choose the correct starting point in the activities for your child, here is a guide to what you can help them develop at different ages. You'll find five milestones for each age group, all of them focusing on the key learning areas.

0–3 months

Motor skills: While lying on the tummy, holds up the head and pushes up on the arms.

Problem-solving: While lying on the back, visually tracks moving objects from side to side.

Communication: Turns head towards noises and voices.

Creativity: Enjoys social interactions, especially using facial expressions.

Independence: Is able to open and close hands.

3–6 months

Motor skills: Begins rolling from front to back and back to front.

Problem-solving: Uses both hands to play and explore a range of toys and objects.

Communication: Uses babbling to gain attention.

Creativity: Enjoys playing with a variety of objects, shapes and textures.

Independence: Brings hands and objects to the mouth.

6–9 months

Motor skills: Picks up small objects with thumb and finger (pincer grip).

Problem-solving: Explores objects of different sizes, shapes, textures and weights.

Communication: Participates in two-way conversations through babbling and various noises.

Creativity: Enjoys playing with musical instruments and colourful objects.

Independence: Moves and reaches to get a desired toy.

9–12 months

Motor skills: Uses thumb and finger to pick up tiny objects, and can release them into a container with a large opening.

Problem-solving: Points to people or objects when named by an adult.

Communication: May start to repeat simple words and sounds, developing longer strings of gibberish.

Creativity: Enjoys a repertoire of songs; moves and claps with enjoyment.

Independence: Can begin to use utensils when eating, and knows tastes that they like and dislike.

12–18 months

Motor skills: Stacks objects on top of one another.

Problem-solving: Beginning to sort objects by size, colour or genre, e.g. cars and animals.

Communication: Combines sounds and words with simple gestures, e.g. waves to say hello and goodbye.

Creativity: Beginning to enjoy a range of sensory materials, e.g. paint and rice, through play without putting them in their mouth.

Independence: Begins to help with dressing and undressing.

1½–2 years

Motor skills: Can use a variety of tools, e.g. cutlery, crayons, paintbrushes, toothbrush, tweezers and tongs.

Problem-solving: Recognises some colours and shapes, and is beginning to count in sequence.

Communication: Joins in with repeated phrases and rhymes from favourite books and nursery rhymes.

Creativity: Beginning to make marks with meaning during creative activities, e.g. This scribble is a fish.

Independence: Begins to enjoy helping with household chores, e.g. laundry, putting things in the bin.

2–4 years

Motor skills: Uses a variety of tools, such as scissors and pencils, with increasing control.

Problem-solving: Understands that objects can be counted, and begins to count independently during play activities.

Communication: Becomes interested in different sounds and words, and is able to build verbal sentences to communicate freely.

Creativity: Becoming increasingly interested in different colours and textures during creative tasks; likes to explore different ways of doing things.

Independence: With adult supervision, can begin to prepare and cut food for mealtimes and participate in baking activities.

4–5 years

Motor skills: Can independently use a variety of tools with control, e.g. a pencil with pincer grip, and scissors.

Problem-solving: Can combine groups to find the total in addition and subtraction activities.

Communication: Has an increasing interest in the words and sounds around them.

Creativity: Participates in crafts and activities, and enjoys a desired outcome. Begins to take care and time when using creative tools, e.g. crayons or pencils.

Independence: Beginning to take necessary safety precautions, such as stopping at the kerb, and understands the risks of unsafe environments.

TOP TIPS

- Timing is *everything*. Never try to engage your little one in an activity if they or you are hungry or tired. It will never end well, and it might not even begin well.
- Preparation is key. If you have an activity up your sleeve, your day will pan out *way* better than if you didn't.
- Tell stories. Storytelling never fails to grab a child's attention. If you think your little one is losing interest, change the story.
- Planned activities are a parenting tool. Use the tool for moments in the day you know can be challenging. For example; around 4pm is always a difficult time for us, I'm usually preparing dinner, the kids are a little tired and getting hungry. This is the perfect time to have an activity 'up your sleeve'; 9 times out of 10 it will save the day.
- During all sensory and messy play activities, put on some gentle classical music. This helps to keep the mood calm, and the whole experience therefore becomes more relaxing for all of you.

BABY PLAY

The 60 activities you will find in this book can be adapted for children aged 1–5, and I offer clear instructions about how to do this at the end of each activity. However, some of the activities are also suitable for babies under a year old, so look out for the symbol shown on page 18.

Play is hugely important for healthy brain development, so the earlier you start playing with your little ones, the better. Here are some fun and simple activities you can do with your baby.

Nursery rhyme time

Never underestimate the value of talking and singing to your baby. Try changing your tone, volume and pitch when you do so, as this will work to enhance your baby's speech and their listening and attention skills. 'Wind the bobbin up' has always been a favourite in our house. We add actions, use whisper voices and make it super-fast. It's guaranteed to make your baby smile.

Once upon a time...

It's never too early to read to your baby. Board books are great for little hands, so show them and let them play with them. Turn pages together and look at the pictures. From as young as birth, you can begin to tell stories to your baby – hearing your voice is their favourite thing. Books help to enhance your baby's visual and cognitive skills, while helping them to learn new language and social skills. Story time can also be a success without a book – use some stuffed animals and create a little show for your baby. They will love it!

Tummy time

You can start tummy time from birth, as the earlier you begin, the quicker your baby will become used to it. Laying your baby on their tummy helps to build muscle strength and will help them to meet major milestones, such as rolling over, sitting and crawling. Try placing some toys, books or coloured scarves in front of your baby – these will attract them and entice them to hold their head up.

Massage time

Massage is the perfect way to comfort and bond with your baby. It is a calm moment between the two of you. A little massage every day can help to ease things, such as colic and reflux. Try some soothing touches and exercises, such as leg raises, bicycle legs, hand and foot strokes and shoulder raises. There's lots of advice available online, and you may even find a local class to attend – it's a perfect first class for parent and baby.

Kick out time

Lay your baby on their back and let them explore. Kick out time encourages freedom and is a great opportunity for them to explore their hand–eye coordination and body movements. Try adding a tracking game while your baby is on their back. Hold a toy or object in front of them, get their attention and move the object from side to side. This encourages your baby to track the object with their eyes, which helps with visual development.

Flying time

Place your baby tummy-down on your forearm, with their chin resting in your hand. Ensure you are fully supporting their weight. Your baby should be able to hold their head up and move their arms and legs freely. Now move your baby up and down, side to side and around the room like an aeroplane. This is a fantastic game to help stimulate your baby's senses and body awareness.

Wriggle time

Music is a great way to play and bond with your baby, but you don't always have to listen to nursery rhymes. Put on some music that you enjoy, and dance in front of your baby; they will love watching you move around the room, following you with their eyes and even wriggling themselves. Also try holding your baby to your chest as you dance together. They will enjoy listening to the music and feeling the rhythmic movements of your body.

Bubble time

Everyone loves bubbles, right? However, babies especially love them. Try blowing bubbles while your baby is lying on their back or sitting with support. They will love watching the bubbles travel through the air, and will enjoy tracking them with their eyes and attempting to grasp them.

Sensory time

As the name suggests, sensory activities encourage babies to use all of their senses. You can try to incorporate sensory time into your weekly routine right from birth. Start by offering some scarves of different colours and textures to encourage them to grasp and explore. As your baby builds up strength on their tummy, try introducing different textures, such as a foil blanket. Babies love foil blankets because they crinkle and scrunch when touched, and are also reflective. Sensory time can evolve as your baby grows.

Copycat time

Try copying your baby and seeing if they notice or repeat the action or sound again. For example, copy a babbling sound your baby makes, or a movement of their hand, and see if they copy you. Gradually start adding new sounds and movements for them to copy. This can be done as soon as your baby starts to become more aware of you and your facial expressions and sounds, at roughly 3–4 months old.

Peekaboo time

Cover your face with your hands, a cloth or scarf, or hide behind an object, such as a sofa or chair. After a moment, come out from your hiding place and say, 'Peekaboo!' This game is great for teaching your baby about object permanence – the idea that something is there, even though they can't always see it. The game can also evolve into hide and seek as your little one grows.

I-spy time

You can play 'I-spy' with your baby from the time they are a few months old. They may not be able to guess the answers, but they will be listening and taking in everything you are saying. This is great for developing a baby's communication skills through verbal recognition. Try saying, 'I-spy with my little eye something that looks like a...cup, ball, plate,' etc. You can play this game with your baby right up until they are speaking, and it will help to develop their vocabulary later on.

ANIMALS

EARTH IS HOME to 8.7 million species of animal, and I think we probably own that number of toy animals too. Our house is bursting at the seams with them.

Learning about the world, its inhabitants and the environments around us is hugely important and beneficial to children. Learning about animals and how we can care for them instils a sense of responsibility and respect for life. Animals also help to teach our children empathy and an understanding of the circle of life.

Before embarking on this theme of activities, you might wish to arrange the animals into groups – safari, farm, zoo, arctic, nocturnal and so on. If, like me, you have an animal-fanatic child, you can make this animal theme last for weeks on end.

Through the next five activities you will be able to immerse your children in tasks relating to a variety of different animals, building curiosity and a desire to find out more. Enjoy learning and researching together. With 8.7 million species, you could really fill your days with lots of animal fun!

Animal Fossils

Make a batch of salt dough fossil bones with your child, then ask them to match the bones to the picture outlines – great fun!

Preparation & instructions

1 Preheat the oven to its lowest setting while you prepare the salt dough with your child.
2 Roll or press the dough out about 1cm (½in) thick, then break off pieces and press them into circle and oval shapes.
3 Get your child to push a different animal into each piece of dough to make imprints.
4 Place the shapes on a baking sheet and dry in the oven for 3 hours, turning them halfway through. Alternatively, leave to air-dry for 2 days.
5 When ready, fill the tray with your chosen material, add the baked fossils and get playing!

Through the ages

AGE 1+ Play hide and seek with the fossils in the tray. You name the animal and prompt your toddler to make the animal sound.

AGE 2+ Prompt your child to name the animal and match the toy animal to the fossil.

AGE 3+ Become an archaeologist and use a paintbrush. Name different parts of the animal's body.

AGE 4+ Can your child start to group animals into mammals, fish, birds etc? Try hiding the initial letters of the animal names in the sand and hunt for those too.

AGE 5+ Using the internet or a book, can your child find out any facts about the animals? Write the animal names on slips of paper, then hide them in the sand and get your child matching them to the fossils.

what you need

- Salt dough (see page 172)
- cookie cutters (optional)
- toy animals
- tray filled with Taste-safe sand (see page 173)
- paintbrush
- plastic letters
- pen and slips of paper
- magnifying glass (optional)

Once upon a time... *woolly mammoths roamed the Earth. They looked like hairy elephants, but they have become extinct. All we have left of them are a few fossilised bones. Today we are going to make our own fossils so that someone else can find them in the future.*

Shirley the Sheep

Shirley needs some wool and she wants it to be of the rainbow kind! A super-fun and colourful activity.

Preparation & instructions

what you need

- pen
- cardboard or clear sticky-back plastic (self-adhesive plastic sheet)
- cotton wool balls (cotton balls)
- glue stick or PVA glue
- gel food colouring
- paintbrushes or pipettes

1 Using the template on page 186, draw the outline of a sheep on some cardboard or sticky-back plastic.
2 Give your child some cotton wool balls and help them to stick the balls on the sheep outline. Give older children a glue stick to do this.
3 Add drops of food colouring to jars of water, then use the paintbrushes or pipettes to add drops of colour to the cotton wool.

Through the ages

AGE 1+ Draw a sheep on some sticky-back plastic. Peel off the backing paper and let your toddler go crazy with some cotton wool balls. The sticky-back plastic makes this a super-fun activity that can be completed more than once.

AGE 2+ Stick cotton wool balls onto the sheep, then use a paintbrush to drip coloured water onto each ball.

AGE 3+ Stick cotton wool balls onto the sheep, then use a pipette to drip coloured water onto each ball.

AGE 4+ Prompt your child to tear the cotton wool balls into tiny pieces before sticking them down. Use the pipette to add some colour (control is key here, as each tiny ball will need just one drop of colour).

AGE 5+ Prompt your child to unwind the cotton wool balls to make spirals. Each spiral will look just like a sheep's wool.

Once upon a time... there was a field of beautiful woolly sheep. Each of the sheep had a thick woolly coat, except for Shirley, who had been sheared. Can you give Shirley a thick woolly coat to warm her up? Add some rainbow colours to make her the most beautiful sheep in the field.

Sponge Footprints

Here's a super-simple stamping activity that can be enjoyed over and again.

what you need

- sponges, about 1cm (½in) thick (potatoes can be used instead, but they will spoil)
- glue gun
- cardboard
- paint, mud, shaving foam or water
- paper
- toy animals

Preparation & instructions

1 Cut out various footprints from the sponges and glue them onto cardboard.
2 Provide your little one with some different textures, such as paint, mud or shaving foam, and get them to dip the stampers in them to make prints.
3 Explore the shapes and talk about who they could belong to.

Through the ages

AGE 1+ Simply print and play. Use water and brown paper for a mess-free activity. Tell your toddler which animal each footprint belongs to. *Key vocabulary: dog, duck, bird, mouse*

AGE 2+ Print and play and get your child to match the footprint to a toy animal. *Key vocabulary: big, small, deer, bird, mouse*

AGE 3+ Can your child make prints with the stampers and then with the toy animals? What's different about them? *Key vocabulary: pointy, sharp, tiny, huge*

AGE 4+ Can your child begin to discuss size and shape? Which is largest? The smallest? Does that tell us about who the footprints might belong to? *Key vocabulary: largest, biggest, smallest, smaller, larger*

AGE 5+ Print with different textures and talk about how they look different. Can you go for a walk in the woods and see if you can find any other footprints? *Key vocabulary: hoofs, webbed, claws, talons, pads*

Question time...

Uh-oh! I left the door open while we were out and have found these footprints. Who put them there? Who do you think has been in our house? Who do these footprints belong to? Let's find out.

Harold the Hedgehog

This activity is not only great for problem solving, it's also a fantastic fine motor activity, working on your little one's muscles in their fingers and hands.

Preparation & instructions

what you need

- coloured pens
- cardboard box
- cocktail sticks (toothpicks) or halved cotton buds (cotton swabs)

1 Using the template on page 186, draw a hedgehog onto a box.
2 Punch some holes into its back.
3 Provide your little one with the box and the cocktail sticks or cotton buds (it is personal preference whether you feel that cocktail sticks are safe for your child and at what age, but play should *always* be supervised, no matter what age). Ask your child to poke the sticks through the hedgehog's back to give him his prickles.

Through the ages

AGE 1+ Show your toddler how to push the sticks through the holes. This is great for hand–eye coordination and learning the pincer grip, which involves coordinating thumb and index finger to pick up an object.

AGE 2+ Can your child poke the cocktail sticks through each individual hole?

AGE 3+ Can your child make their own holes with the cocktail sticks?

AGE 4+ Show your child that more than one cocktail stick will fit into the larger holes, and get them to practise changing the number of sticks according to the size of the hole.

AGE 5+ Look at the different amounts of sticks needed; can they count and compare amounts?

Once upon a time...
there was a hedgehog called Harold. Like all hedgehogs, Harold went out at night to find food, but one day he overslept. When he went out it was daylight and all kinds of animals began swooping down on him. To protect himself he tried to use his spikes, but they had disappeared. Can you give Harold back his spikes?

Mrs Crabby Claws

This activity takes a lot of coordination and concentration but it's great fun and strengthens the hand muscles for skills such as holding a pencil.

Preparation & instructions

what you need

- coloured pens
- cardboard
- scissors
- glue gun
- 2 clothes pegs (clothes pins)
- large pom-poms or tissue paper balls
- sticky labels

1 Using the template on page 187, draw a crab on some cardboard and colour it in.
2 Now cut out the claws, and cut each of them into two separate parts.
3 Using a glue gun, stick each half of the claw on either side of the peg, where it opens above the spring.
4 Glue just *one* handle of the peg (the part below the spring) to the arm of the crab.
5 Set out lots of pom-poms and practise collecting them with the claws. For older children, you can write letters on labels, stick them to the pom-poms and ask them to catch particular sounds.

Through the ages

AGE 1+ Show your toddler the crab and tell them the story. Can they collect the pom-poms by hand?

AGE 2+ Can your child collect the pom-poms and sort them into colours? Practise the pincer grip, prompting them to use thumb and index finger to pick up an object.

AGE 3+ Practise opening and closing the claws – can they move one at a time? Can your child grab the pom-pom of your choice? Ask them to grab a certain colour, or stick a letter onto each of the pom-poms and ask them to find a specific sound.

AGE 4+ Can your child use both claws at the same time? Can they collect any of the balls? Can they make any words with the lettered pom-poms once they have caught them?

AGE 5+ Can your child collect two lettered balls at the same time? You could focus on two letters that come together to make one sound, such as sh, ch, th, ng.

Once upon a time...
Mrs Crabby Claws was very cross. Some little crabs from across the road had been throwing balls into her garden. Can you help Mrs Crabby Claws to remove all the balls?

BUGS

CHILDREN ARE NATURALLY curious and inquisitive about the world and all living things. My boys are never alone in the garden – they always have a pet snail or worm to look after. By exploring insects, their habitats and nature, you are allowing children to make sense of the world around them. You are also providing huge opportunities for your children to learn how to care for and respect living things, and opening up a world of curiosity.

Encourage your children to explore outside. How many insects can they find? What could they discover if they turned over a large rock? What insect might be hidden in the mud?

Here are five bug activities that you can enjoy with your child. Before each one, go for a wander in your garden or local park and see if you can find the bug linked to each task. Seeing a real butterfly before making your own can really add to the magic of craft.

Sun-Catcher Butterfly

Butterflies come in all shapes, colours and sizes. They are perfect for exploring creativity with different patterns, colours and textures.

Preparation & instructions

what you need

- pen
- cardboard or paper
- craft knife
- clear sticky-back plastic (self-adhesive plastic sheet) or sticky tape
- tissue paper, paint, flowers, petals, leaves, pom-poms, beads, cellophane … whatever you have to hand

1 Using the template on page 181, draw the outline of a butterfly onto cardboard or paper.
2 Cut out different shapes inside the wings.
3 Add a sheet of clear sticky-back plastic to the back of the butterfly.
4 Prompt your child to stick colourful items to the clear areas to create a beautiful sun-catcher.

Through the ages

AGE 1+ Let your toddler paint a piece of paper, exploring the different colours and textures. Once dry, place your stencilled butterfly over the painting to reveal a beautiful pattern on the wings.

AGE 2+ Choose three colours of tissue paper and show your little one how to rip it into small pieces. Stick the tissue paper into the cut-out areas.

AGE 3+ Choose five or six colours to identify. Can your child complete a pattern on each wing, e.g. red, blue, red?

AGE 4+ Collect a range of natural resources, e.g. flowers, petals, leaves. Identify the colours and discuss the different shades. Fill in the cut-out areas on the wings.

AGE 5+ Collect a range of natural resources, e.g. flowers, petals, leaves. Initially prompt your child to fill in just one wing. Can they match the second wing to make a symmetrical butterfly?

Once upon a time...

there was a beautiful butterfly called Beatrice. One morning, Beatrice woke up, looked into the mirror and gasped. She had lost her pattern; her once beautiful symmetrical wings were bare. Where had her pattern gone? What can you do to help her?

Tweeze the Spots

A fun-filled fine-motor activity with playdough and pom-poms – what more could you need? Introduce your child to Larry the Ladybird (Ladybug) and spark a conversation about his spots. Have fun adding and removing the spots on Larry's back again and again.

Preparation & instructions

what you need

- pen
- cardboard or paper
- red Playdough (see page 172)
- wooden spoon
- pom-poms or black beans
- children's tweezers

1 Using the template on page 179, draw an outline of a ladybird on a piece of paper or cardboard.
2 Make or source red playdough and add to the ladybird outline to create the body.
3 Use the handle of a wooden spoon to poke dents in the playdough.

Through the ages

AGE 1+ Have fun with your toddler adding pom-poms to the dents in the playdough and removing them with their fingers. Pushing and digging little fingers into playdough is a perfect fine motor work out.

AGE 2+ Push the spots into the ladybird as far as they can go.

AGE 3+ Give your child a pair of tweezers to remove the spots from Larry's back.

AGE 4+ Place two spots, one on top of the other, in each dent. Can your child use the tweezers to remove both spots at the same time?

AGE 5+ Begin to count the spots and see if your child joins in. Which side of the ladybird has the most spots? Which side has the least? How many would you have left if you took three spots away?

Once upon a time...
there was a ladybird called Larry. Can you say hello to him? Larry is feeling very sad. What do you think could be making him feel sad? Larry went for a walk in the woods and somehow managed to find more spots. Can you help to remove some of Larry's unwanted spots?

Copycat Bugs

Copycat drawing is great for developing a child's speaking and listening skills. It is also a fabulously quiet and calm activity. Put on some children's classical music, dig out your pens and start drawing together.

Preparation & instructions

what you need

- paper
- crayons or felt-tip pens or paint sticks

Complete the steps below, explaining and drawing at the same time, then ask your child to copy. Remind them to take their time. Children sometimes lose themselves in their creativity, so simple reminders can bring them back to the task in hand.

1 Draw a yellow circle.

2 Colour it in.

3 Add three black lines.

4 Make a dot for the eye.

5 Add two small circles at the top of the big circle – these will be the wings.

6 Draw a small triangle on the bottom as a 'stinger'.

Through the ages

Making marks on paper is a *huge* developmental stage, especially if your child can tell you what it is supposed to be. Don't worry what it looks like; the aim of this activity is speaking, listening and attention.

AGE 1+ Select the colours you will need for a bumble bee. Draw some simple shapes and see if your toddler can copy. *Key vocabulary: yellow, black, circle*

AGE 2+ Can your child name the colour? What shapes can they see? Show them how to draw some simple shapes and ask them to copy. *Key vocabulary: circle, triangle, line, dot, leg, wing*

Listening time...

Today we are going to learn how to draw a bumblebee. It is your job to listen very carefully to my instructions. It's my turn, then your turn, but never together. (Repeat this sentence each time you draw one part of the bug. The idea is the child watches, concentrates, then copies. Both you and your children will feel like you have achieved something amazing at the end of this drawing practice.)

AGE 3+ Follow steps 1–3 above. Can they add anything else to make the bee look more lifelike? *Key vocabulary: wing, leg, middle, larger, smaller*

AGE 4+ Follow all the steps, then draw a dotted line from the back of the bee in the shape of any letter. Explain that a bee has made some lines on the paper. Can your child trace over the lines and tell you the letters and sounds? *Key vocabulary: larger, smaller, on top of, underneath, centre*

AGE 5+ Ask your child to create their own step-by-step instructions for you to follow. Can they use their own language to describe how to draw an insect?

Spaghetti Worms

Cooked spaghetti is a brilliant sensory base – a fantastic texture for children to explore. It's also great for imaginative play and builds curiosity.

Preparation & instructions

what you need

- Rainbow cooked spaghetti (see page 175)
- Taste-safe mud (see page 173)
- large tray and towel (optional)
- bowls, cups, bottles
- children's tweezers or kitchen tongs

1 Prepare the Rainbow spaghetti in as many colours as you like, and make the taste-safe mud.
2 To reduce the clean-up process, you can set up this activity in an empty bath. When you've finished, just remove the spaghetti and drain the mess away with water. You could also do this activity in a tray or in the garden.

Through the ages

AGE 6 MONTHS+ Messy, taste-safe play can be enjoyed even at this age. Poke your rainbow spaghetti through the holes in a colander. Your baby will have lots of fun trying to pull out the worms.

AGE 1+ Place the rainbow spaghetti in a tray and mix well with the taste-safe mud. Prompt your toddler to use the pincer grip (thumb and index finger) to pick up the worms.

Once upon a time...
deep in the Rainbow Jungle there lived a family of worms. Some were long, some were short, but all of them were brightly coloured. Have fun exploring all the different kinds of worms you can find.

AGE 2+ Using their hands or fingers, can your child pick up the worms and put them into the small opening of a bottle? This will work on their hand–eye coordination.

AGE 3+ Provide your child with children's tweezers or tongs and ask them to place the worms one by one in a tray. Do they notice the length of the worms?

AGES 4–5 Provide your child with a pair of children's tweezers and ask if they can pick up each worm and place it in a bottle.

Bug Count

Cardboard and plastic bottle caps are all you need to make this counting activity. Each little ladybird (ladybug) can have any number of spots you want. Your child simply adds the correct number of beans to the corresponding ladybird.

Preparation & instructions

what you need

- glue gun
- up to 12 red plastic bottle caps
- cardboard
- pen
- dried black beans

1 Using a glue gun, stick your bottle caps to a piece of cardboard (see photo).
2 Draw a head and some legs around each cap to create 12 little ladybirds, or however many you like depending on the age of your child.
3 Write a number above each of the ladybirds.
4 Supply your child with black beans to pop into the caps.

Through the ages

If your child still explores by placing things in their mouth, partly cook the black beans before use. This will ensure that the activity is safe for them to explore in whatever way they choose.

AGE 1+ Provide your toddler with two ladybirds and a small bowl of 12 black beans. Can they place a bean inside each ladybird? Can they place more beans inside each ladybird and say which one has the *most* and which one has the *least*?

AGE 2+ Provide your child with five ladybirds and some black beans. Can they count each of the ladybirds? How many are there? Explore the beans together.

AGE 3+ Provide your child with all 12 ladybirds and some black beans. Can they count each of the ladybirds? How many are there? Explore the beans together.

Once upon a time...
in the middle of a deep dark forest, there was a special school. This school was for ladybirds. In Class 3D, there were 12 loud, lively ladybirds all wishing they could count! Can you help them?

AGE 4+ Provide your child with all 12 ladybirds and some black beans. Can they count out the correct number of beans and place them inside the correct ladybird?

AGE 5+ Provide your child with all 12 ladybirds and some black beans. Label the ladybirds in twos (2, 4, 6, 8, etc.) so that the twelfth ladybird is labelled with the number 24. Talk about *odd* and *even* numbers, and how you can *double* a number. Double one is two, and so on.

DINOSAURS

DINOSAURS ARE PRETTY EPIC! I remember the first time I learnt that dinosaurs had once existed and I was in complete shock. Their extraordinary size and mysterious disappearance create wonder and awe, spark curiosity and create endless opportunities for discussion about the past and present. They open our eyes to an unknown world of peculiar beasts, giant creatures and strange lands. It's no surprise, then, that dinosaurs can spark imagination like no other topic.

Here are five activities that even a dinosaur novice can enjoy. Have fun researching, learning and digging for facts about these awesome creatures.

Dinosaur Sensory Bottles

Sensory bottles, also known as calm bottles, are a brilliant resource for children of all ages. Babies from 3 months onwards *love* them, and they are also good for children who are struggling with their emotions.

what you need

- plastic bottles
- fillings, e.g. stones, flowers, leaves, water beads, paper clips, pipe cleaners, magnetic letters
- small dinosaur toys (choosing some in similar colours to the flowers makes them more difficult to find)
- water
- vegetable oil or baby oil
- glue gun or superglue

Top tip: *Use these bottles during transitions through the day, such as playtime to dinner time. For example, say, 'Grab one of our special dinosaur bottles to explore while we eat.' This simple tool has stopped a lot of tantrums in our house.*

Preparation & instructions

As an example, let's make a flower bottle.

1 Fill the bottle with brightly coloured flowers and leaves.
2 Add the dinosaurs.
3 Half-fill the bottle with water.
4 Top up the bottle with oil.
5 Glue the bottle cap in place.
6 Shake the bottle and play.

Through the ages

AGE 3 MONTHS+ Make the bottles for your baby. Place your baby on their front for tummy time and let them explore the bottles. They will love watching the bubbles and different colours.

AGE 1+ Involve your toddler in collecting different materials and filling the bottles together. Being involved in making the bottles will make them even more fascinating.

AGE 2+ Sensory bottles are a calming resource for helping toddlers deal with their BIG emotions. Make them together and let them have a go at pouring in the water.

AGE 3+ Add some paper clips, pipe cleaners or magnetic letters, and explore the bottle with a magnet on the outside. Watch as the magnetised bits float up and down. Can your child make them move past the dinosaurs? Can they find the hidden letter?

AGE 4+ Play around with the water/oil ratio – what difference does it make? Talk about and explore the way the oil and water separate. Name the dinosaurs you can spot in the bottle and find out some facts about them during a quiet time.

Dino Slime

Please stay with me here, because this slime is like no other. It's messy, but not as messy as conventional slime. It's also taste-safe, non-toxic and incredibly easy to clean up. Let me introduce you to chia seed slime, the coolest texture ever. Pop it in a tray, add some dinosaurs, scoops and bowls and enjoy a cool sensory experience!

what you need

- Chia seed slime (see page 173)
- tray
- toy dinosaurs
- pom-poms
- spoons, scoops and bowls

Once upon a time... millions of years ago, dinosaurs ruled the land. Some were enormous, some were very fierce, but one, called Danny, was a very mischievous diplodocus. His favourite thing was to stomp in a swamp. He loved getting his huge legs stuck in the sticky swamp and would always shout for help. What a naughty dinosaur!

Preparation & instructions

1 Put your slime in a tray and add some dinosaurs.
2 Try adding some coloured pom-poms for the dinosaurs to play with – it's so much fun trying to get them out of the slime.

Through the ages

AGE 1+ Explore the strange texture of the slime. Your toddler might not like it straight away, so offer them a scoop if they prefer not to handle it.

AGE 2+ Enjoy pulling the dinosaurs from the slime. It is very malleable, but easily flows back into liquid form, so explore rolling it into balls.

AGE 3+ Provide spoons and scoops and watch how your child takes on the challenge of filling their bowl. This is great for those hand muscles.

AGE 4+ Can your child cover the dinosaur in the slime? Can they get all the slime off? Can they move all the slime from one bowl to another? This sounds super-simple, but it can be difficult!

AGE 5+ Can your child play around with the different measurements in the recipe? What happens when you add more water? What happens when you add more cornflour?

Excavation

Who wouldn't want to be a palaeontologist for the day? This activity might look complicated, but it's very easy to put together, and even easier to execute. You just make a batch of salt dough, mould it into dinosaur bones, place them in a tray of sand and let your child dig to find them.

what you need

- pencil and/or pen
- cardboard
- Salt dough (see page 172)
- Taste-safe sand (see page 173)
- tray
- paintbrush

Listening time... Today you have a very special job: you are going to become a palaeontologist – someone who digs up dinosaur bones! We have been sent an exciting package all the way from Portugal. The package is marked Fragile because it contains the bones of an amazing dinosaur called an Allosaurus. Can you help to put the dinosaur bones back together?

Preparation & instructions

1 Using the templates on page 190, draw the dinosaur outline onto two sheets of cardboard.
2 Preheat the oven to its lowest temperature while you make the salt dough with your child.
3 With your child (depending on age), place bits of dough on the various stencilled dinosaur bones and mould into a matching shape.
4 Place the bones on a baking sheet and dry in the oven for 3 hours, turning them halfway through. Alternatively, leave to air-dry for 2 days.
5 Make the taste-safe sand and place it in a tray.
6 Once the bones are cool, hide them in the sand-filled tray.
7 Provide your child with the cardboard stencils.
8 Prompt them to dig around in the tray to find the hidden bones.
9 Use the paintbrush to brush off the sand, then match each bone to the correct outline on the stencils.

Through the ages

AGE 1+ Make different-sized bones and place them in a tray of taste-safe sand for your toddler to find and explore. *Key vocabulary: big and small*

AGES 2–3 Select 2–6 bones and prompt your child to put them in the correct place on the dinosaur stencils. *Key vocabulary: name the different body parts, e.g. leg, arm, skull*

AGES 4–5 Work together to mould the different bone shapes on the stencils. Put each of the bones in the correct place on the stencils. Discuss the different information you can find out about an allosaurus. *Key vocabulary: allosaurus, bone names, e.g. skull, spine, pelvis*

Pegasaurus

Introducing maths into a play activity is the best way to explore numbers. It makes maths stress-free and fun!

Preparation & instructions

what you need

- pencil
- cardboard
- paint or coloured pens
- scissors
- 20–25 clothes pegs (clothes pins)
- pom-poms in colours that match the dinos

1 Using the templates on page 188, draw five dinosaurs onto cardboard.

2 Cut out the dinosaurs, then paint or colour them in five different colours with your child.

3 Don't forget to number the dinos 1–5.

4 Collect some pegs (I use coloured pegs so that we can match peg colour to dinosaur), five of each colour and number the pegs 1–5.

Through the ages

AGE 1+ Practise matching colours, using pom-poms instead of pegs.

AGE 2+ Match the pegs to the same-coloured dinosaur, and help your child to open and close the pegs. Can your little one count?

AGE 3+ Can your child order the pegs from 1 to 5? Can they add the correct amount of pegs to match the number?

AGE 4+ Can your child order the dinosaurs from 1 to 5, match the colour pegs and put the pegs in the correct numbered order?

AGE 5+ Add a piece of clear sticky tape to each dinosaur to create a wipeable area. Using a wipe-clean marker, write a sequence of numbers in the taped areas, e.g. 3, 4, 5, 6, 7. Can your child arrange the numbers from largest to smallest? Can they notice any missing numbers?

Once upon a time...
there was a family of five rainbow-coloured dinosaurs. They all had spikes on their backs, but these spikes were very special. The dinosaurs could take them on and off, and they could swap them. Stacey the stegosaurus loved everything to match, so can you help to match the coloured spikes to the right dinosaur?

Dino Eggs

With my children, this activity ended up as an *epic* science experiment. We made loads of eggs across a whole week, hiding a small toy dinosaur in each one. We then made predictions about which dino would be in which egg, and worked together to crack them open and see if we were right. This will honestly keep children entertained for hours.

Preparation & instructions

what you need

Choose the egg you want to make according to the age of your child (see below) and you will see which of the listed ingredients is needed. Of course, you could make all the eggs if you like!

- Sand playdough (see page 172)
- small toy dinosaurs
- ice-cube tray and water
- bicarbonate of soda (baking soda), water and gel food colouring (optional)
- bowl of vinegar mixed 50/50 with water
- Salt dough (see page 172)
- hammer (optional)

Once you have chosen the egg you want to make, prepare the ingredients for it and make it with your child.

Through the ages

AGE 1+ *Sand playdough* – wrap the dough around a toy dinosaur, forming it into an egg shape, and watch your toddler break it open to find the dino inside.

AGE 2+ *Ice* – place some tiny toy dinosaurs in the compartments of an ice-cube tray and cover them with water. Place in the freezer until solid. Provide your child with some salt and warm water to help each dinosaur escape its egg.

AGE 3+ *Bicarbonate of soda (baking soda)* – to make one egg, mix 120g (1 cup) bicarb with 1 teaspoon water, adding a spot of food colouring if you like. Mould this paste into an egg shape around a toy dinosaur. Wrap in clingfilm and freeze overnight. To reveal the dinosaur, provide your little one with a bowl of diluted vinegar and prompt them to put the egg in it. Watch as the egg fizzes and a little dinosaur is revealed.

AGE 4+ *Salt dough* – mould the dough around a toy dinosaur to form an egg shape. Place on a baking sheet and dry in an oven preheated to its lowest temperature for 2 hours, turning it halfway through. Alternatively, leave to air-dry for 2 days.

AGE 5+ For the most epic science experiment, spend the week making each of the different eggs above. Then make a chart and write down your predictions about which dino is in each of the eggs. Will they be easy to crack open? What should you use? Will you be successful? How long will it take?

Listening time... At present over 700 different dinosaurs have been named and identified. Each type of dinosaur came from a different type of egg – some were huge, some were small. What different kinds of dinosaur eggs can you find?

MUSIC

HAVE YOU EVER noticed how children pick up a tune or some lyrics really easily? Research has shown that newborn babies can even remember tunes and sound sequences heard while in the womb... how amazing is that?

Musical activities always have a way of engaging, distracting or changing a child's mood. From as young as 18 months, children naturally become more tuneful as they develop more control over vocal sounds and rhythms.

We can introduce music into our homes in lots of ways, but a good starting point to explore different sounds and instruments is to add music to playtime. Whenever we engage in a messy play activity, I put on calming children's classical music. In my experience, it helps to keep my children engaged for longer, keeps the play calm and introduces them to sounds they wouldn't necessarily hear day to day. It's always a winner!

Here are five fun DIY music activities to get your children exploring sounds. Each instrument is made from things you'll have around your home.

Rain Stick Bottle

Rice is a brilliant music maker. Add some sticks and rice to a plastic bottle, turn it this way and that, and watch the rice take a journey around the sticks, making wonderful sounds as it travels up and down. Sing the song with your child while playing with your rain stick. Try passing your rain stick back and forth from one another to practise taking turns.

Preparation & instructions

what you need

- sticks
- plastic bottle
- dried rice
  (for Rainbow rice, see page 175)

1 Go on a hunt in your local park or woodland and collect sticks of different lengths.
2 Put a few sticks in your bottle, trimming the long ones to fit.
3 Add some rice (plain or rainbow-coloured).
4 Put the lid on the bottle and you're all set!

Through the ages

AGE 3 MONTHS+ Place the bottle on the floor in front of your baby during tummy time. Turn it upside down and let them watch and listen to the sound it makes.

AGE 1+ Have fun collecting sticks together and ask your toddler to fill the bottle with them. Add the rice and explore the sound it makes.

AGE 2+ Fill the bottle with as many sticks as possible. The rice will have a much harder job to get from the top to the bottom.

AGE 3+ Have fun making a range of different rain sticks. What changes can you hear in the sound when you add more or less rice? What happens if you add more sticks or remove some?

AGE 4+ Try using different-sized bottles to see how it changes the sound.

Nursery-rhyme time...
Rain, rain go away
Come again another day.
Mummy wants to play
(Repeat the verse with a different name each time.)

Rubber Band Guitar

You'll get the most wonderful sounds from this simple musical instrument. The cardboard guitar is completely optional. Enjoy some nursery-rhyme time, taking it in turns to sing along and pluck the strings as you do so.

Preparation & instructions

what you need

- rubber bands
- loaf tin or cake tin
- cardboard, pen, scissors and glue (optional)

1 Stretch some rubber bands around the tin and pluck the strings. The tin helps to give the strings a much more authentic sound.

2 If you want to make the tin look like a real instrument, try drawing and cutting a guitar out of cardboard. Stick it onto the tin with dots of glue.

Through the ages

AGE 1+ Try adding only two strings to the tin and show your toddler how to pluck each of them. Sing along together.

AGE 2+ Add three strings to the tin and prompt your child to pluck them one by one. Can they copy your sequence?

AGE 3+ Add five strings to the tin and practise plucking them along with the song. One pluck for each of the letters in B-I-N-G-O.

AGE 4+ Sing B-I-N-G-O, but with each verse miss out one of the letters. Prompt your child to pluck only when you sing one of the letters.

AGE 5+ Play copycat BINGO. Match each of the letters in BINGO with a different colour string. Pluck that string each time you sing the letter. E.g. B is pink, I is orange and so on.

Nursery-rhyme time...
There was a farmer who
   had a dog,
And Bingo was his
   name-o.
B-I-N-G-O!
B-I-N-G-O!
B-I-N-G-O!
And Bingo was his
   name-o.

Drum Set

Tin-can drums make the most wonderful sound ever! Create a drum set and sing along together, using your hands or sticks to bang the drums, each of which can make a variety of noises.

Preparation & instructions

what you need

- empty tin cans
- balloons
- rubber bands

1 Set out your clean tin cans.
2 Cut off the neck of a balloon (the part you blow into).
3 Stretch the balloon around the open end of a can.
4 Place a rubber band around the can.
5 Explore all the different sounds it can make by banging and plucking.

Through the ages

AGE 7 MONTHS+ When your baby is able to sit unaided, place a drum in between their legs and watch them explore the different sounds it makes.

AGE 1+ Enjoy exploring the drum set. Bang the drums along to the song. *Key vocabulary: bang, boom*

AGE 2+ Explore the words fast and slow. Enjoy banging along to the music, changing the tempo for your child to copy. *Key vocabulary: fast, slow*

AGE 3+ Begin to explore pitch by plucking the rubber band without holding the tin can. Now try turning the can upside down and plucking again. *Key vocabulary: pitch, high, low*

AGE 4+ Prompt your child to repeat a tune that you make. Hit the drums in a sequence, changing the tempo and pitch. *Key vocabulary: pitch, tempo, high, low, fast, slow*

Nursery-rhyme time...

The ants go marching one by one, hurrah, hurrah
The ants go marching one by one, hurrah, hurrah
The ants go marching one by one,
The little one stops to suck his thumb
And they all go marching down to the ground
To get out of the rain, BOOM! BOOM! BOOM!
(Sing extra verses, e.g. 'The little one stops to tie his shoe/ climb a tree/shut the door'.)

Glass Jar Xylophone

My children absolutely love this activity, which is brilliant for all ages! Fill a range of glass jars with varying amounts of water, then tap on each one with a stick to make a beautiful sound. The general rule is that the less water and more space in the jar, the deeper the sound it makes. The space determines the amount of vibration, which is what sound is made from!

Preparation & instructions

what you need

- water
- glass jars of different sizes
- sticks or wooden spoons
- gel food colouring (optional)
- toy xylophone

1 Pour some water into your jars. Start with a full jar and work your way down to an empty jar.
2 Tap each jar with a stick and you will hear it make a different sound.
3 Add colours to the water if you want to make the jars look more exciting.

Through the ages

AGE 1+ Explore the different sounds and sing along to 'Twinkle, twinkle'.

AGE 2+ Listen to the different sounds and try to match your vocal sounds to the high and low sounds made by the jars. We always sing, 'High, high, high, low, low, low'.

AGE 3+ Play a tune on the toy xylophone and ask your child to repeat it back to you on their jar xylophone. Start simply with two different sounds and work up to more.

AGE 4+ Try to match the jar sound to the xylophone sound by adding or removing water from a jar. (Do this little by little – slow and steady wins this race.)

Nursery-rhyme time...
Twinkle, twinkle little star
How I wonder what
* you are.*
Up above the world
* so high,*
Like a diamond in the sky.
Twinkle, twinkle little star,
How I wonder what
* you are.*

Tambourine

You have to do a little advance preparation for this activity, but it's such a great instrument, and made with recyclables. Simply shake and bang along to the song.

Preparation & instructions

what you need

- drill or screwdriver
- 16 plastic bottle caps
- pen and round side plate
- cardboard
- hole punch
- string or ribbon

1 Use a drill or screwdriver to make a hole in each of the bottle caps.
2 Draw two circles on cardboard (I drew around a side plate), then cut them out.
3 Using the hole punch, make 8 equally spaced holes around both circles, keeping them 2cm (¾ in) from the edge.
4 Thread some string or ribbon through each hole.
5 Thread two bottle caps (inside facing each other) onto each string and tie the ends – not too tightly, as you want the caps to rattle.

Through the ages

AGE 1+ Explore the different sounds the tambourine makes and sing along to 'Down in the Jungle'.

AGE 2+ Prompt your child to stamp their feet and bang the tambourine at the same time.

AGE 3+ Move your body and bang the tambourine on different body parts. What different sounds can you hear?

AGE 4+ Shake, bang, dance and sing along using the tambourine. Prompt your child to add their own verses to the song, e.g. 'There's a little baby *monkey* washing his clothes'.

Nursery-rhyme time...
Down in the jungle where nobody goes
There's a little baby elephant washing his clothes.
With a scrub-a-dub here
And a scrub-a-dub there
That's the way he washes his clothes.
(Sing extra verses, inserting a different animal each time.)

NATURE

WHENEVER WE ARE having a particularly tough start to the day, I get everyone dressed and head outside. Being in nature has a way of making everything seem better. It clears your head, relaxes you and naturally helps you to breathe more easily.

Learning with nature gives children huge physical, emotional, intellectual and social benefits, so try to factor in a nature walk as often as you can. Being around nature provides children with the experience of a free-flowing and ever-changing environment that stimulates all the senses.

Children are born scientists, and nature provides endless opportunities for developing inquisitive minds, fostering creativity and taking risks.

Each of the activities in this topic encourages you to explore the natural world, find hidden treasures and bring them home to create a fantastic learning opportunity.

Nature Bunnies

You can create pretty much any picture you like with leaves and petals. Try making the bunny shape shown here, and perhaps turn it into a beautiful card for a loved one with the words, 'Some bunny loves you'.

Preparation & instructions

what you need

- selection of leaves
- paper
- pen
- glue
- scissors

1 Go on a nature hunt and find a variety of leaves in different colours and shapes.
2 Grab the other items listed and you're all set to create.

Through the ages

AGE 1+ Draw an outline of a bunny, cover it in glue, snip up all the leaves and get your toddler to stick them on.

AGE 2+ Arrange a selection of leaves in the shape of a bunny and draw around it. Remove the leaves, then prompt your child to stick them in the correct place (like a puzzle).

AGE 3+ Mirror sticking – you stick one leaf down and prompt your child to copy.

AGE 4+ Prompt your child to create their bunny and to use the remaining leaves to add some grass and a tree.

AGE 5+ Give your child a pair of scissors and prompt them to cut different shapes out of the leaves to add detail, such as eyes and whiskers, to their bunny. They can also use other items, e.g. flowers, feathers, to add detail.

Question time...

What does it mean to be kind? Discuss how you can show kindness, e.g. sharing, giving a hug, asking someone to play, saying kind words. Can they remember a time someone said something kind to them? Let's make a card for someone we love. Can you think of something kind to say to that person?

Sunflower Craft

Can your child glue some pasta onto cardboard to create a beautiful sunflower? Build on that creativity and help their fine motor skills by getting them to add sunflower seeds and remove them using tweezers.

Preparation & instructions

what you need

- pen and round side plate
- cardboard
- scissors
- glue
- dried pasta quills
- sunflower seeds
- children's tweezers

1 Draw a circle about 10cm (4in) in diameter on cardboard, cut it out and paint it brown.
2 Pierce holes all over the circle.
3 Stick this circle onto an A4 (US letter) size piece of cardboard and add a stalk and a few leaves.
4 Set out bowls of pasta and sunflower seeds, and get ready for fun!

Through the ages

AGE 1+ Prompt your toddler to stick the pasta around the cardboard circle, like petals.

AGE 2+ Create your sunflower and leave to dry. Once dry, prompt your child to pop a seed into each of the holes in the centre of the sunflower.

AGE 3+ Create your sunflower, slot the seeds into the centre and prompt your child to use some tweezers to remove each of them.

AGE 4+ Prompt your child to create a pattern with the pasta. Can they use different pasta shapes to create a different effect? How many sunflower seeds can they remove?

AGE 5+ Prompt your child to complete simple equations using the seeds. E.g. 3+3=?

Once upon a time...
on a hot summer day in a field far away, there stood hundreds of giant sunflowers swaying in the breeze. They all had bright yellow petals, apart from one. One sunflower stood tall and proud, but it was completely bald, with not even one petal. Can you add some yellow petals to this sunflower?

Nature Scavenger Hunt

Here's a super-simple scavenger hunt, made with cardboard and pegs, that will give a focus to any short trip out and about. Get your child to draw some pictures of common nature treasures that they usually find on a walk. Can they find each of the items on the list and peg them onto the board?

Preparation & instructions

what you need

- cardboard
- pen
- clothes pegs (clothes pins)
- glue gun

1 Talk to your child and ask what they love to find when they go to the woods or the park.
2 Depending on their age, draw or list some of the objects on a piece of cardboard.
3 Next to each item, glue a clothes peg.

Through the ages

AGE 1+ Choose some simple familiar objects to find. Go for a walk and help your toddler to spot these treasures. *Key vocabulary: flower, stick, leaf, grass*

AGE 2+ Ask your child to recall some objects they might find in the woods or park. Go for a walk and help them to spot these treasures. *Key vocabulary: feather, pine cone, stone*

Once upon a time...
there was a little girl called Sophie who wanted to go on an adventure. She packed a bag with binoculars, a magnifying glass, scissors, a compass, a whistle and a torch and she made a list of all the beautiful treasures she would like to find on her journey. What treasures would you like to find on your adventure?

AGE 3+ Can your little one help you to make a list of all the things that you can find in the woods or park? Now can they find them with minimal help? *Key vocabulary: dandelion, tree bark, clover, berries*

AGE 4+ Can your child draw some of the familiar objects they might find on a nature walk? While on your walk, prompt them to describe each of the objects for you to find. *Key vocabulary: descriptive language, such as prickly, soft, smooth, rough*

Shape Finders

Sticks can create the best wands! These shape wands are perfect for children of all ages. You can use them to spark imagination or to find shapes in the natural world.

Preparation & instructions

what you need

- sticks
- pen
- cardboard
- scissors and craft knife
- glue gun
- string or ribbon (optional)

1 Grab some sticks. We found ours in the woods, but you could use bamboo sticks or lolly (popsicle) sticks.
2 Draw and cut shapes on cardboard, like those shown in the picture, giving them a window in the centre.
3 Using a glue gun, stick a cardboard shape to each stick. Tie some pretty string or ribbon around them if you like.

Through the ages

AGE 9 MONTHS+ Take your baby for a walk in the buggy. Give them a shape finder and show them how to hold it up and peer through it. Name all the objects you find together.

AGE 1+ Use your shape finder and go on a mission to look through it to find different objects. Name those objects as you play.

AGE 2+ Using one shape finder at a time, go on a hunt with your child to find as many things of that shape as possible.

AGE 3+ Take all your shape finders and go on a shape hunt in your local area. What different shapes can you find? Can you play I-spy with your shape finder, using the beginning sounds of words?

AGE 4+ Make a huge hunt in your garden or local park. Write some letters and/or numbers on different-shaped slips of paper, hide them and get your child to use their shape finders to hunt these down.

Question time...

Shapes are all around us. Everything is made up of different shapes. The sun looks like a giant circle or sphere, a fence is a rectangle and road signs and traffic cones are triangles. What different shapes can you see?

Leaf Monsters

Finding leaves has never been such fun as in this activity! Go on a leaf hunt and try to find the biggest leaves you possibly can. Then have some fun giving them eyes and faces. We loved playing around with different emotions for each of the leaves.

Preparation & instructions

what you need

- selection of large leaves
- felt-tip pens (we used metallic pens to make the expressions show more clearly)
- googly eyes
- glue

1 Gather lots of leaves.

2 Grab your pen pot, some googly eyes and glue and start creating monster faces!

Through the ages

AGE 1+ Have fun adding some googly eyes to your leaves.

AGE 2+ Can your child guess how each of the leaves is feeling once you have drawn a face on it?

AGE 3+ Can your child draw some simple faces?

AGE 4+ Prompt your child to draw a range of different faces on the leaves. Can they tell you a story as to why each leaf is feeling that way?

AGE 5+ Display your leaf monsters. Prompt your child to find the face that shows how they are feeling.

Once upon a time...

there was a town full of leaves. Each leaf looked completely different from the others. There was a grumpy leaf, a happy leaf, a sad leaf, an excited leaf, a bored leaf, a naughty leaf and an extremely cheeky leaf. Can you add a face to your leaf and tell me how they are feeling?

OUR BODIES

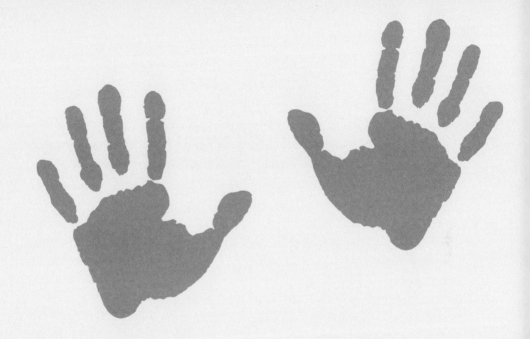

TEACHING BODY AWARENESS is super-important – it helps children to learn about healthy eating and exercise for life. It teaches them to take care over what they eat, and helps them to make the right choices independently.

As soon as my children started eating, I would tell them the health benefits of certain foods. It sounds like a silly notion to tell a 6-month-old baby about the food they are eating, but a simple sentence such as, 'Oh, this is a delicious healthy carrot' is enough. Now my son is 4 years old, he knows what food gives him the most energy (carbohydrates), which ones make his bones strong (calcium in milk and yoghurt) and even what makes his brain healthy (omega-3 in fish).

Body awareness runs deeper than talking about what we consume, so here are five activities to teach children about their bodies and their feelings. I hope they will provide you with the tools and opportunities to open up deeper conversations with your own little ones.

Billy's Body

It might look complicated, but this craft is just a box lid, a drawing and some bones and organs cut out of cardboard. Remember, whatever you make does not have to be a masterpiece!

Preparation & instructions

what you need

- pencil
- cardboard
- coloured pens
- scissors
- children's tweezers

1 Using the template on page 182, draw a body, complete with X-ray rectangle, on a piece of cardboard and colour it in.
2 Using the templates on page 183, draw some bones and organs on another piece of cardboard and cut them out. You can colour these too if you like.
3 Supply your child with some tweezers and prompt them to guess the correct places where the bones and organs should go.

Through the ages

AGE 1+ Draw an outline of a body. Together, can you name the different body parts, e.g. legs, arms, head, etc? Can your toddler place a pom-pom on each of the body parts when you name them?

AGE 2+ Draw an outline of a body. Separately draw some body parts – hands, feet, head, neck, etc. Can your toddler put the parts in the correct place?

AGE 3+ Focus on either bones or organs. Can you teach your child the proper names and put them in the correct place using tweezers?

AGE 4+ Arrange the pieces in the wrong places for your child to correct. It's quite challenging to pick up and hold thin cardboard, but it's great for strengthening the fingers.

Question time...

Billy needs help to put his bones and organs in the right place. Where do his lungs go? What job do the lungs do for the body? Where does Billy's heart belong? What is the heart's job? What is the correct name for the bones? Pelvis, spine, ribcage, etc. Can your child name anything else that belongs in the body?

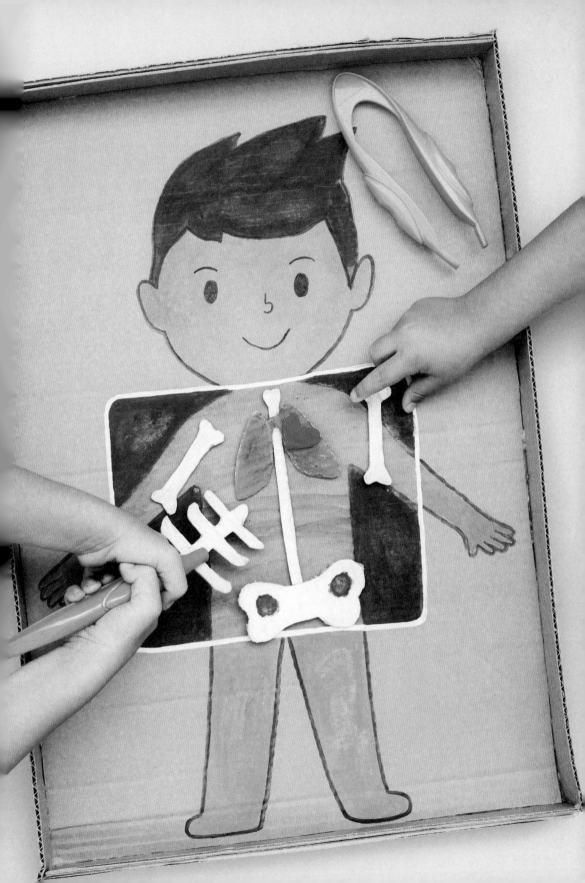

X-Ray Craft

You won't believe how a hand outline, some flour and cotton buds can provide so much fun. You can stick this craft down to keep, or just play around with the cotton buds (no flour) to keep it mess-free, it's completely up to you.

Preparation & instructions

what you need

- black paper
- paintbrush and water
- flour
- cotton buds (cotton swabs)
- scissors

1 Gather everything you need.
2 Cut five of the cotton buds into three pieces.
3 Get your child to place their hand on a piece of black paper and go around it with a wet paintbrush.
4 Sprinkle flour over their hand, then ask them to remove their hand and brush off any flour still on the back of it.
5 Give your child the cotton buds, keeping the long ones separate from the short ones, and show them how to create a hand X-ray.

Through the ages

AGE NEWBORN+ Have fun taking your baby's hand print once a month to see how they've grown over their first year of life.

AGE 1+ Make a handprint picture with your child. Use just water on brown paper for a mess-free option, or use paint for a keepsake. Compare both your handprints.

AGE 2+ Draw around your child's hand on some black paper and get them to draw or paint inside the shape.

AGE 3+ Paint around your child's hand with water and dust with flour. Provide some cotton buds and ask where they think the bones in their hand are.

AGE 4+ Show your child an X-ray image you've made of a hand. Can they recreate it?

Once upon a time...
there was a little girl called Judy, who loved to dance. One day, whilst dancing, she hurt her finger. The doctor told Judy that they needed to X-ray her hand. Can you make your own X-ray to show Judy?

AGE 5+ Tell your child that there are 19 bones in one
hand and give them exactly 19 bones of different
lengths. Can they recreate a hand, guessing where
all the bones go?

Emotion Stones

This is such a simple way to get your children talking about how they are feeling, and understanding more about different emotions. Find me a child who doesn't love playing with stones!

Preparation & instructions

what you need

- stones
- pen
- cardboard

1 Collect some flat stones, the bigger the better.
2 Using the template on page 180, draw an outline of a person on cardboard.
3 Draw faces on the stones to show different emotions.
4 Arrange the stones around the outline, and there you have it – a tool for talking about big emotions.

Through the ages

AGE 1+ At this age, children express themselves mainly by smiling, laughing or crying. Use the words happy, sad or excited to describe their emotions. This is the beginning of their journey in emotional intelligence. *Key vocabulary: happy, sad, excited*

AGE 2+ Talk about feelings, such as happy, sad, scared, excited and angry with your child. Can they tell you what makes them happy and sad? *Key vocabulary: happy, sad, scared, excited, angry*

AGE 3+ Look at feelings, such as happy, sad, scared, excited, angry, shocked and tired. Can your child give you an example of when they felt these things? *Key vocabulary: happy, sad, scared, excited, angry, shocked, tired*

AGE 4+ Look at some more complex emotions, such as feeling worried. Together, unpick some different emotions. Sharing your own examples is always helpful before asking your child to share.

Once upon a time...

there was a girl called Dolly. Dolly had a lot of BIG emotions and sometimes found it tricky to tell people how she was really feeling. Sometimes Dolly shouted. Sometimes she screamed, and sometimes she cried. Dolly needs help to understand about all the different ways we can feel. Can we help Dolly and teach her about different emotions?

Healthy-Eating Harry

This a fun way of sparking conversations about what we put in our bodies. Be cautious about what food and drink you label as unhealthy. It's important to give children the same advice you give yourself. Everything is okay in moderation.

what you need

- pen
- cardboard
- craft knife
- selection of real food (Try this activity on the day you do your food shop and play it before you put everything away.)

Once upon a time...

there was a boy called Harry, who ate lots of silly things. He ate books and toy cars, sponges and soap. One day, his daddy decided it was time that Harry learnt about healthy eating, so he went to the kitchen and put lots of different foods on the table. Can you help Harry and his dad decide which foods are healthy or unhealthy? Feed Harry all the healthy food.

Preparation & instructions

1 Using the template on page 189, draw a picture of Harry on a large piece of cardboard.
2 Give him a huge open mouth, or cut a large hole where the mouth should be.
3 Place your selected foods in front of the picture.
4 Tell your child that this is Healthy-Eating Harry and he is not allowed any unhealthy food. Can they feed Harry the correct food?

Through the ages

AGE 1+ Collect a range of fruits and vegetables and have fun posting the food through the hole in the picture. Continually use the word 'healthy'.

AGE 2+ Split the food into healthy and unhealthy. Focus on only a few unhealthy foods. Count the foods in each group. Which one has the most?

AGE 3+ Look at different groups of food, e.g. fruits and vegetables. Count the food in each of the groups. Which one has the most and least?

AGE 4+ Begin to look at a range of food groups, such as carbohydrates, dairy, meat, nuts, seeds, etc.

AGE 5+ Can your child create a healthy balanced meal for Henry to eat? Discuss different food groups and what is important for our bodies to thrive.

Brush Your Teeth

We absolutely love playing this activity, and anytime my boys start to show hesitance with tooth brushing, we grab this out of the cupboard and play.

what you need

- coloured pens
- cardboard
- clear sticky-back plastic (self-adhesive plastic sheet) or sticky tape
- wipe-clean marker pens
- shaving foam
- toothbrush

Preparation & instructions

1 Using the template on page 183, draw a picture of a mouth, gums and teeth on a large piece of cardboard and colour it in.
2 Cover the whole picture with sticky-back plastic or sticky tape.
3 Using wipe-clean markers, make some marks on the teeth to indicate food, plaque and grime.
4 Grab some shaving foam and a toothbrush and get brushing!

Through the ages

AGE 1+ Show your toddler how using the shaving foam and toothbrush will wash away any marks on the teeth. Sing the song while you brush.

AGE 2+ Get your child to add some dirt and marks to the teeth. Have fun washing them all off with the toothbrush and foam.

AGE 3+ Add a new level of learning to this play by writing some letters on the teeth and asking your child to brush off different letters. Do this one at a time.

AGE 4+ Add a range of letters and numbers to the teeth and get your child to brush them off, one at a time.

Nursery-rhyme time...
This is the way we brush
our teeth, brush our
teeth, brush our teeth.
This is the way we brush
our teeth, so early in the
morning.
Brush 'em up, brush 'em
down, in little circles,
round and round.
This is the way we brush
our teeth, so early in
the morning.

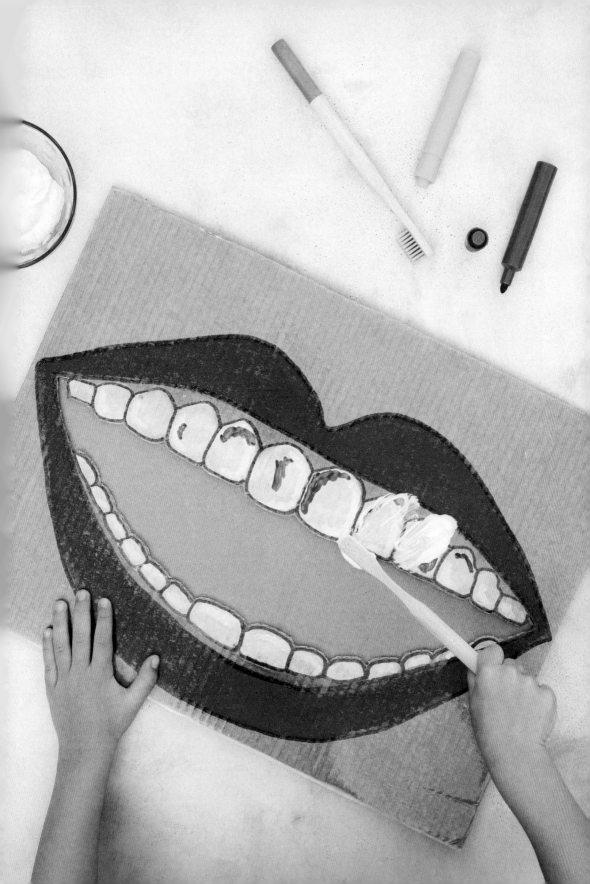

COLOURS

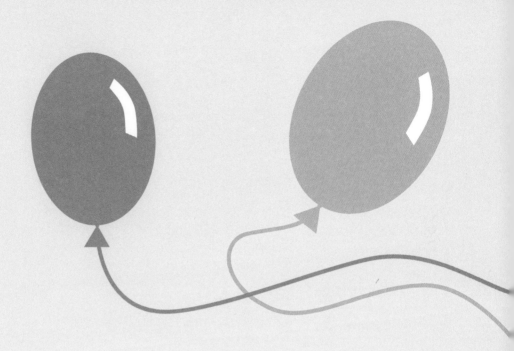

OUR WORLD IS literally filled with colours, so learning about them is essential for children to explore the world we live in. We use colours to categorise and describe everything. Children will notice, for example, that one car is blue and another is yellow. By teaching them colours as early as possible, you are providing them with the verbal skills to describe and enjoy the world around them.

Of course, it would be impossible to teach colour without talking about rainbows. Children love them, and when you think about it, rainbows are pretty magical: an arch of colour suddenly appears in the sky when the sun is shining and rain is in the air. Just imagine how a child must feel when they see a rainbow for the first time. It must blow their minds!

Here are five activities (including two specifically about rainbows) to help you and your child explore colour and to sort, categorise, compare and organise.

Posting Machine

A cardboard box has never been such fun! You can even get your bigger kids designing and making their own posting machine.

Preparation & instructions

what you need

- pen or pencil
- 6 toilet roll tubes
- cardboard box
- craft knife
- coloured sticky tape, dots or paper, or paints
- glue gun
- 6 plastic bottle caps, plus the screw part they fasten to
- coloured lolly (popsicle) sticks and pom-poms

1 Draw around one end of a toilet roll tube to make two circles on three sides of the box (six circles in total). Use a craft knife to cut out the circles.
2 Cover each cardboard tube and bottle cap in coloured tape (it's the quickest way to add colour).
3 Push the tubes a little over halfway through the holes. Glue the caps to the front of the box as shown in the photo.
4 Set out the lolly sticks and pom-poms for your child to post.

Through the ages

AGE 1+ Practise posting. Can your toddler post a pom-pom through a tube? Focus on the pincer grip.

AGE 2+ Begin matching the colours. Which colour pom-pom or stick belongs where? Prompt your toddler to name all the colours.

AGE 3+ Using six different letters, label the tubes and bottle caps, one letter per colour, e.g. 'S' on the red bottle cap and red tube. Can your child match the correct letters and colours?

AGE 4+ Label each bottle cap and cardboard tube with a different letter. Can your child match them all?

AGE 5+ Prompt your child to make a posting machine to their own design, with this great junk modelling game to which you can then add a learning activity. E.g. try making a spout for vowels and a spout for consonants.

Once upon a time...
there was a street called Colour Crescent. Every summer, there was a huge sports day and all the colours took it very seriously. The reds were the fastest runners and the blues could jump the highest. This year, can you help to organise all the colours into their teams? Which colour will be first?

Puffy Paints

Puffy paints are absolutely awesome, and so easy to make. Your child will love exploring the texture and colours.

what you need

- coloured pens
- cardboard
- clear sticky-back plastic (self-adhesive plastic sheet) or sticky tape
- shaving foam
- cupcake tray
- gel food colouring (red, yellow, blue)
- paintbrushes
- yoghurt (just for babies)

Nursery-rhyme time...
Red and yellow and pink and green,
Purple and orange and blue.
I can sing a rainbow,
Sing a rainbow,
You can sing one too!

Listen with your eyes,
Listen with your eyes,
And sing everything you see.
You can sing a rainbow,
Sing a rainbow,
Sing along with me.

Preparation & instructions

1 Using the template on page 187, draw a rainbow on cardboard and colour it in.
2 Cover the whole picture with clear sticky-back plastic or sticky tape.
3 Put some shaving foam in each compartment of a cupcake tray.
4 Place tiny amounts of food colouring in each cup, combining them as necessary to make all seven colours of the rainbow. A little goes a long way.
5 Give your child a paintbrush to colour in the rainbow with puffy paint.

Through the ages

AGE 6 MONTHS+ Mix plain yoghurt with food colouring to make all the colours of the rainbow. Explore the texture and colours with your baby. Complete a painting together. Make sure to take a photo!

AGE 2+ Make the puffy paints and explore them at bath time. This is a great way to introduce your toddler to the new texture and mess, and allows for a quick clean-up afterwards.

AGE 3+ Provide your child with a rainbow to colour in. Prompt them to choose the correct colours. Which colour comes first? If they find this tricky, show them a picture for reference.

AGE 4+ Provide your child with different images to colour. Can they choose the correct colour for each item in the pictures?

AGE 5+ Set your child a challenge to mix two colours together. What new colour do they make?

Rainbow Rice

Rice is one of the best sensory materials to play with because it has a great texture and also makes a lovely noise. Your child will really enjoy the scooping, pouring, filling and emptying involved.

Preparation & instructions

what you need

- Rainbow rice (see page 175)
- bowls or jars
- scoops or spoons
- paint and/or gel food colouring
- 6 toilet roll tubes, cardboard and glue (optional)

Hook a fitted sheet around your table legs or chair legs to trap the mess and allow for an easier tidy-up.

1 Make your rainbow rice in several colours and place each colour in a separate container.
2 Set out some empty bowls or jars along with some scoops or spoons.
3 Make a DIY pouring station as shown in the photo. Paint the toilet roll tubes, cut an archway at the bottom of each tube and glue the tubes to a piece of cardboard. You can then position this *above* the bowls so that the rice pours into them.

Through the ages

AGE 1+ Prompt your toddler to explore the rice and its texture. Name all the colours and prompt them to copy. *Key vocabulary: pink, blue, green*

AGE 2+ Provide your child with a spoon and a container and let them practise filling and emptying. Talk to them about the words full and empty. Name the colours of the rice together. *Key vocabulary: pink, orange, yellow, green, blue, purple*

AGE 3+ Provide your child with several containers and play around with filling up, emptying and comparing. *Key vocabulary: full, empty*

AGE 4+ Explore filling, emptying and comparing. Give your child instructions, e.g. add three scoops of green rice to the container. Which container has the most? *Key vocabulary: most, least*

Question time…

Which container has the most? Which has the least? Which colour is your favourite? How many more scoops will you need until it is full? Are any of the tubes full? Are any of the tubes empty? Can you add three more scoops to the green container? Why does it make that sound when it falls?

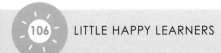

Eat the Rainbow

Here is a visual tool to encourage your children to eat more fruit and vegetables. Just add a coloured pom-pom to the drawing each time your child eats a fruit or vegetable in a colour of the rainbow.

what you need

- pens or paints
- cardboard
- rainbow-coloured pom-poms

Nursery-rhyme time...
I like to eat, eat, eat
  apples and bananas.
I like to eat, eat, eat
  apples and bananas.

I like to eat, eat,
  eat sweeties and
  chocolate.
I like to eat, eat,
  eat sweeties and
  chocolate.

I like to eat, eat, eat
  spinach and carrots.
I like to eat, eat, eat
  spinach and carrots.

(Try adding your own foods
to this song to bring some
laughter to your day. Chat
about whether those foods
are healthy or unhealthy.)

Preparation & instructions

1 Using the template on page 187, draw a rainbow on some cardboard, then colour it in.
2 Grab some rainbow-coloured pom-poms and away you go.
3 Explain to your child that fruits and vegetables come in all the colours of the rainbow. When you eat them, they fill your body with lots of goodness that makes you fit, strong and healthy.
4 As an extra activity, take your rainbow to the supermarket and get your child to find some fruit and vegetables that match each of its colours.

Through the ages

AGE 1+ At each mealtime, show your toddler their rainbow and see if they can match any of their food with its colours. Tell them what colour they are eating. This is a great way to bring lots of language to the dinner table.

AGE 2+ During each meal, talk about what you are eating. Can your child name each of the foods on their plate? What colours can they see? Add a pompom to the rainbow to match the food on their plate.

AGE 3+ Begin talking about the taste of foods – can your child make comparisons? Can they talk about what foods are their favourites and why? Add a pompom to the rainbow to match any food on their plate.

AGE 4+ Discuss and discover the goodness in food. Begin to talk about why certain foods make us healthy and strong; which foods are better for us and why? Ask your child to add pom-poms to the rainbow to match the foods on their plate.

Tip: This activity aims to give your children the opportunity to talk about their food in a variety of different ways, and gives them the independence to choose the right foods for their bodies.

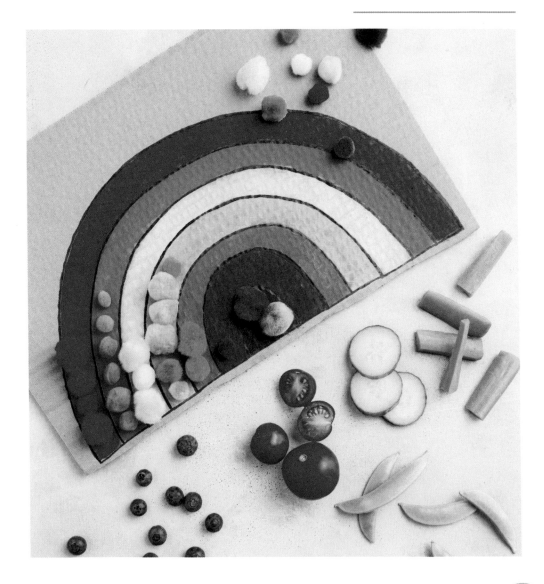

Adding Machine

Making maths fun is the most important thing we can do when exploring numbers and shapes. This activity does just that. You simply pop some counters into each tube and count how many end up in the bowl. Addition is really that easy!

Preparation & instructions

what you need

- Rainbow pasta (see page 175)
- paint
- 2 cardboard tubes
- glue gun
- cardboard
- small cardboard box or disposable bowl
- black pen
- clear sticky tape
- wipe-clean marker pens
- tray

1 Dye your pasta in several colours and leave to dry overnight.
2 Paint the cardboard tubes in the same colours as the pasta and leave to dry.
3 Glue the tubes to a sheet of cardboard. Glue a small box or disposable bowl underneath the tubes.
4 Using a pen, draw a square beside each tube and cover each one with clear sticky tape – these are your wipeable areas, where you can write the numbers for each sum in wipe-clean markers.

Through the ages

AGE 1+ Explore and play with the rainbow pasta.

AGE 2+ Post pasta down the two tubes. Look at how the two lots come together in the bowl to make one group. The concept of addition really can be *that* simple.

AGE 3+ Work together to answer different sums. Discover the simplicity of addition, and revel in the fact that your 3-year-old is adding!

AGE 4+ Prompt your child to answer number sums independently and to recognise numbers 1–10.

AGE 5+ Discover doubling. Look at what happens when you add a number to itself. Discuss odd and even numbers.

Once upon a time...

there was a little girl called Annie, who loved numbers, but she often got in a muddle. A fairy appeared and said, 'I am the number fairy, here to help you.' She waved her magic wand and an amazing machine appeared. 'This will solve all your problems,' she said.

SEASONS

I LOVE THE changing seasons, each and every one. People always ask, 'Do you prefer summer or winter?' 'What about spring and autumn?' I respond. Autumn is my favourite time of year. I love the colours, the falling leaves and the crisp, blustery mornings.

Seasons are also my favourite thing to teach because they are all around us and can be taught continuously. A simple glance out of the window can provide children with 10 questions that they want to find the answers to.

By providing our children with the opportunities to go out and explore the seasonal changes, we are allowing them to observe nature, question the passing of time and understand the sometimes subtle differences in the world around us.

We can learn about the seasons in a variety of ways, but through play is the most fun! Four of the following five activities cover a different season, and one covers them all. Have fun looking for those beautiful changes that are just outside your door.

Blossom Tree

This is one of our favourite springtime activities, and there are so many ways you can do it. Here we explore five of them!

Preparation & instructions

what you need

- paper
- paints
- cotton buds (cotton swabs) and rubber band or sticky tape
- brown pen
- cardboard
- cotton wool balls (cotton balls)
- clothes peg (clothes pin)
- scissors
- bubble wrap
- pink tissue paper

1 Gather everything you will need.
2 For children aged 1–2, work with paper and paint.
3 For older children, draw a brown branch on a piece of cardboard, then work with the materials as suggested for each age.

Through the ages

AGE 1+ Explore finger painting with your toddler. Provide some paper and just pink and white paints so that the picture will come out looking beautiful no matter how many fingerprints are added.

AGE 2+ Fasten 5–6 cotton buds together with a rubber band or sticky tape. Prompt your child to dip one end of the bundle in the pink paint and dab it onto a sheet of paper.

AGE 3+ Grip a cotton wool ball with a wooden peg, then dip the ball into the paint and stamp blossoms onto the branch.

AGE 4+ Cut small bits of bubble wrap and dip the bumpy side into the paint. Press it onto the cardboard branch to create beautiful bunches of blossom.

AGE 5+ Pierce holes in the cardboard branch. Now make some blossom flowers: stack five or six sheets of pink tissue paper and cut out simple flower shapes about 10cm (4in) in diameter. Place your finger in the centre of each stacked flower, then grasp that dent underneath and tightly twist it into a point. Push the point of each blossom into a hole in the branch.

Once upon a time...

on a cold spring morning, a little girl named Rebecca went exploring. She noticed that lots of things had changed. The grey sky had white clouds and hints of blue. The bare ground was sprouting flowers, and the trees above her were decorated with sprigs of pretty pink flowers.

Snowmen

Snow isn't just for Christmas. My children love playing with snowmen throughout the year, and it always sparks lots of conversation.

what you need

- Play snow or Taste-safe play snow, depending on age (see page 174)
- tray
- carrot
- black beans or googly eyes

Preparation & instructions

1 Make your snow (getting your children to help if you like), and place it on a tray.
2 Help your children to make some snow figures.
3 Add bits of carrot for the noses.
4 Add black beans or googly eyes for the eyes and buttons.

Through the ages

AGE 6 MONTHS+ Make some taste-safe snow and put it in a sealable plastic bag for your baby to explore. Try taping the bag to the floor so they can explore it during tummy time. You can also add the snow to a clear plastic bottle and let them explore shaking it.

AGE 1+ Make some taste-safe snow and explore the texture together. This snow allows you to mould it into shapes. Also try pouring it into bowls and scooping it up.

AGE 2+ Can your toddler mould the snow into snowballs?

AGE 3+ Prompt your little one to make snowballs and stack them up. This takes patience, resilience and control.

AGE 4+ How many balls can you stack on top of each other without them breaking? Can your child add a carrot nose, plus eyes and buttons to their snow friend? This can be tricky because, if the snow is not compacted enough, it will just crumble.

Once upon a time...

in the middle of an icy winter, stood a lonely snow woman. Although the weather was very cold, there had been only one day of snow, so the children in the street managed to build just the snow woman. She desperately wanted a snow friend. Do you think you could make a friend for her? Will you make another snow woman or a snowman?

Weather Wheel

Here is an activity tool that can be used all year round, every day. Can your child move the wheel to show what the weather is today?

Preparation & instructions

what you need

- pencil and 20cm (8in) saucepan lid
- cardboard
- scissors
- ruler
- coloured pens
- split pin

1 Draw around the saucepan lid on a piece of cardboard and cut it out.
2 Using a ruler, divide the circle into eight equal segments and draw a different weather symbol in each one.
3 Place the circle on a large rectangle of card and push the split pin through the middle to join both layers together. Make sure the circle can spin freely.
4 Draw an arrow on the rectangle as shown in the photo.
5 Align the wheel with the arrow to show what the weather is today.

Question time...

What is the weather like today? What colour is the sky? Where is the sun hiding? Can you see any rain on the leaves? Can you see any frost on the ground? If we open the door or window, how will the air feel? What do you think the temperature is like today? What clothes should we wear now we know the weather? What do you think the weather forecast might be for tomorrow?

Through the ages

AGE 1+ Talk to your toddler about the weather every day. 'The sun is shining today.' 'Oh dear, it's raining today.' *Key vocabulary: sun, rain*

AGE 2+ Ask your child what the weather is like today. Show them the weather wheel and get them to match the weather to one of the pictures. *Key vocabulary: cloudy, grey*

AGE 3+ Look at the weather today and describe it. Prompt your child to use more descriptive vocabulary. What colour is the sky? How cold or warm do you think it is? *Key vocabulary: frosty, icy, cold, warm*

AGE 4+ Looking at the weather today, can your child make a decision about the clothes they should wear? Open up a discussion and get them to tell you why they have chosen those particular clothes.

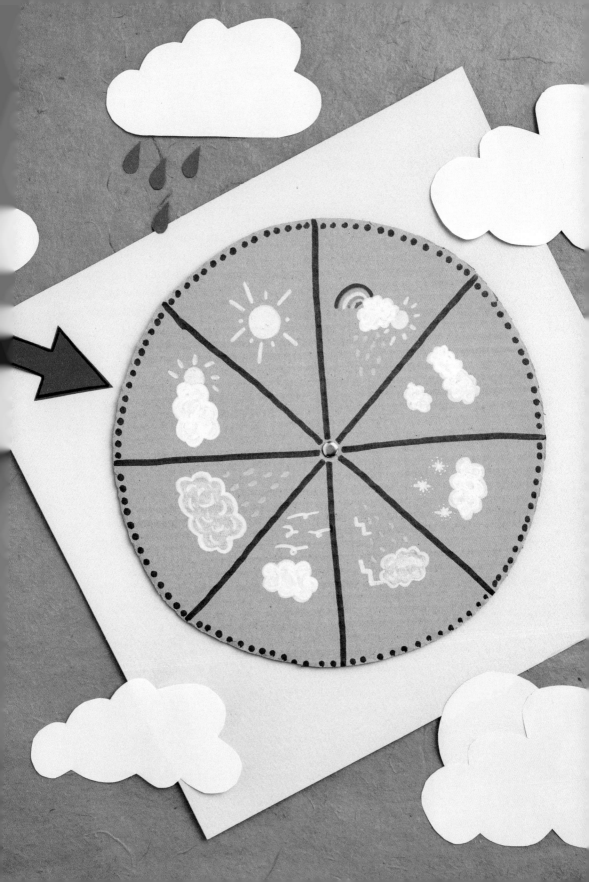

Conker Run

Think of this as a giant ball run that you make together with some beautiful natural treasures and enjoy as a family.

Preparation & instructions

what you need

- scissors
- large cardboard box
- 10 toilet roll tubes
- glue gun
- glue dots or masking tape
- 2 baskets or bowls
- conkers, acorns and pine cones
- ruler or tape measure

1 Trim the cardboard box as shown in the photo – you want one long side and one end flap.
2 Cut eight of the toilet roll tubes in half lengthways.
3 Using a glue gun, stick the halved tubes in a curved shape on the large cardboard sheet, one after another, as close together as possible.
4 Glue the two uncut tubes to the flap, one above each run.
5 Use glue dots or masking tape to fix the cardboard flap to the wall, making sure the runs are angled.

Through the ages

AGE 1+ Make a small ball run; glue a toilet roll tube to some cardboard and lean it against a wall. Show your toddler how to post the conkers down the tube.

AGE 2+ Using the large ball run, watch the conkers, acorns or pine cones travel from top to bottom. Practise counting each conker you post.

AGE 3+ Can your child place a basket at the bottom of each run to collect the conkers? This is harder than it looks, as conkers have a mind of their own. Who has the most?

AGE 4+ Compete against your child. Whose conker will get to the bottom first? Whose conker will travel the furthest?

AGE 5+ Grab a ruler or tape measure and show your child how to measure the distance the conker has travelled. Whose conker travelled the furthest?

Once upon a time...
in an autumn forest, the great woodland Olympics had just begun. All the pine cones gathered around to see who would win the conker race. Would it be Mrs Shiny Conker or Mr Small Conker? Will the smallest conker win gold? The question on everyone's lips was, 'Are acorns really faster than conkers?'

Play Beach

Great for rainy days, this is one of my boys' favourite sensory activities. They both love playing with sand but – disclaimer! – I'm not a fan because it gets everywhere. Using sand playdough, though, they feel like they are playing with sand but it's practically mess free.

what you need

- Sand playdough (see page 172)
- shells (optional)
- tray
- sea animals (optional)
- wooden/foam letters

Nursery-rhyme time...
(To the tune of 'The Wheels on the Bus')

The waves at the beach go up and down, up and down, up and down,
The waves at the beach go up and down, all day long.
The crabs at the beach, crawl back and forth, back and forth, back and forth...

Preparation & instructions

1 Make your sand playdough, involving your children if you like. They will have lots of fun mixing and kneading.
2 Mix in some shells, if you have any.
3 Place the sand playdough in a tray.

Through the ages

AGE 1+ Playdough is fantastic for little hands, but children under 2 need careful supervision so it doesn't end up in their mouths. Get your toddler to practise breaking off chunks of playdough and squidging it between their fingers.

AGE 2+ Make some prints in the sand playdough and get your little one to match up the object to the print (it's just like a puzzle).

AGE 3+ Sensory activities are a great way to incorporate phonics learning. Try adding some letters to the dough and discuss which sounds they find.

AGE 4+ Get your child to print some letters of their own, can they make any of the sounds or even tell you a word that begins with the sound?

AGE 5+ Prompt your child to make some consonant-vowel-consonant (CVC) words by printing the letters in the sand. Words such as; cat, bug, kid, pet, rock.

SPACE

LEARNING ABOUT SPACE sparks imagination and ignites curiosity. Space, planets, the moon and the entire solar system are all fascinating. Why? Because of the unknown, the 'what ifs' and the fascinating questions that lead to learning about outer space. It helps children to become creative thinkers, to challenge current theories and to question uncertainties.

When you were at school, did you learn that there were nine planets? I certainly did. But when I started teaching, we suddenly 'lost' a planet and the total was reduced to eight. What actually happened was that the International Astronomical Union (IAU) decided that Pluto no longer fitted the bill as a planet, so it's now classed as a dwarf planet.

This in itself sparks a load of curiosity and so many questions that I'm inspired to find all the answers myself. Just imagine what learning about space will do for our children's brains.

Here we have five activities to get us thinking and learning about space.

Space Cookies

We bake most weeks in our house, and these space cookies have been a huge hit again and again. They are much simpler than they look and your children will love making them.

Preparation & instructions

what you need

- Shortbread (see page 175)
- 4 tbsp icing sugar (powdered sugar)
- 1 tbsp boiling water
- gel food colouring (black, blue, purple)
- wire rack
- edible glitter (optional)

Remember to use a large ceramic bowl when baking with children; it's too heavy for them to move around and allows for a much 'tidier' baking session.

1 Get your child to help you make and bake your cookies in round and star shapes. Set them aside to cool.
2 Make some icing (frosting) by mixing your icing sugar and water in a shallow dish.
3 Add a few drops of each food colouring to your icing, stirring lightly to create a rippled effect.
4 Place a cookie face down in the icing, twist in a clockwise direction and transfer to a wire rack. Repeat with all the cookies.
5 Sprinkle with edible glitter, if using, and leave to dry.

Through the ages

AGE 1+ Baking with babies can be fun, but it can also be messy. Pre-measure each of the ingredients and let your toddler add them to the bowl.

AGE 2+ Use some cookie cutters to make some shapes. Can your child cut the cookie? Support them to put them on the baking sheet.

AGE 3+ Support your child to add the icing to the cookies independently. Note: it can be tricky to get the biscuit out of the icing.

AGE 4+ Prompt your child with a little guidance and support to follow the decoration steps on their own. They will love the cookies, regardless of how they turn out.

AGE 5+ Give your child directions, but tell them that today they are going to make the cookies all by themselves. Read each step together. You may both be surprised how well the cookies turn out.

Once upon a time...
in a galaxy far, far away, there lived a family of cookie munchers. They ate cookies for breakfast, lunch and dinner, but these were not ordinary cookies. They were special space cookies. Follow this recipe to make some magical space cookies of your own.

Moonscapes

Sensory play is one of my children's favourite kinds of play – it can keep them entertained for hours at a time. The cloud dough you make for it will keep for months if sealed in an airtight container, so you can reuse it time and again.

what you need

- Taste-safe play snow for toddlers, or Cloud dough for older children (see page 174)
- tray
- foil
- pots, bowls, spoons, scoops, cutters
- pen and slips of paper

Preparation & instructions

1 Make the dough, involving your child if you want to. My boys love adding the oil to the cloud dough and seeing it come together.
2 Place the snow or dough in a tray.
3 Roll some bits of foil into balls to make moon rocks.
4 Grab some pots, cups and spoons and away you go.

Through the ages

AGE 1+ Explore the taste-safe dough together. This dough is malleable and can be moulded into balls and containers. It's also brilliant for making marks and patterns. This is one of my favourite sensory bases.

AGE 2+ Using cloud dough, spoons and different utensils, make some moonscapes, adding some foil moon rocks. Ask your little one to press their spoon into the dough to make patterns.

AGE 3+ Write some individual letters (s, a, t, p, i, n) on slips of paper, roll them up and wrap some dough around them to make moon rocks. Hide them in the moonscape and prompt your child to find them and see what they say. Can they read the letter inside? Once they have found them all, lay them out and see if they can make a word from the gobbledygook.

AGE 4+ Hide some simple CVC words, e.g. tap, hut, set, pip, got, inside moon rocks. When your child has found them all, lay the words out and see if you can come up with some funny sentences together.

Question time...

What can you find out about the moon? Is it really made of cheese? What do you think the moon would feel like? Has anyone ever been on the moon? When do you see the moon in the sky? What colour is the moon?

AGE 5+ Write 'The dog sat on the cat' on a piece of paper. Tear it into separate words and hide each word in a moon rock. Can your child find them, read the words and rearrange them to make the hidden message make sense?

Intergalactic Fizzers

Here's a science experiment that never gets old, and it impresses children time and again. When sodium bicarbonate and vinegar mix, they react with each other and make carbon dioxide gas, which results in a fantastic fizz!

Preparation & instructions

what you need

- 200g (7oz) bicarbonate of soda (baking soda)
- 2 tbsp water
- gel food colouring (blue, purple)
- glitter (optional)
- tray
- box or cloth
- pen and paper
- vinegar mixed 50/50 with water
- squeezy bottles or pipettes

Make the space rocks in secret so that your children don't see. The element of surprise will allow for lots more communication.

1 Divide the bicarbonate of soda between two bowls.
2 Mix half of the water with blue food colouring, and mix the rest with purple.
3 Stir the blue into one bowl of bicarb, and the purple into the other bowl.
4 Add some glitter, if you like.
5 Shape two-thirds of each coloured paste into moon rocks and leave to dry.
6 Use the remaining paste to make a spiral shape of moondust on a tray.
7 When the rocks are dry, dot them around the tray.
8 Cover the tray with a box or cloth.
9 Write the note from NASA and away you go.

Story time

Set out a tray of fizzers, cover it and tell your child: 'We have had a very special space delivery and it looks like it has come from NASA! Shall we see what's inside?' Unveil the intergalactic fizzers and read the delivery note.

Through the ages

AGE 1+ Put some diluted vinegar in a squeezy bottle and give it to your toddler. Prompt them to add some to the intergalactic rocks to make them fizz. What is happening? What colours can they see? *Key vocabulary: wow, fizz*

AGE 2+ Give your child a pipette or squeezy bottle of diluted vinegar to make the rocks fizz. What do they notice? What can they smell? What colours can they see? *Key vocabulary: blue, purple*

AGE 3+ Enjoy watching your child explore this science experiment. What do they notice when they add different amounts of vinegar to each rock? What do they think the rocks are made from? *Key vocabulary: more, less*

AGE 4+ While exploring this activity, ask your child what they think is happening. Who is NASA? How do they think the rocks came from space? *Key vocabulary: solid, liquid*

AGE 5+ Explain to your child what is happening – that the two ingredients are reacting. The reason these rocks are 'melting' is because of the reaction and because the rocks do not like carbon dioxide. Research what gases can be found in space. *Key vocabulary: solid, liquid, gas, reaction*

Hello Wise Ones,

We need you to investigate some space rocks.

They landed in the garden of an elderly man who lives in ... (insert your road name).

Please find out if they are dangerous and whether we should be concerned about any more peculiar space rocks appearing.

Report back immediately.

NASA

Shape Aliens

Learning about shapes has never been such fun! All your child has to do is feed the shape aliens the correct shape.

what you need

- pen
- cardboard
- scissors
- craft knife
- googly eyes
- 4 small boxes (multipack cereal boxes are perfect)
- sticky tape
- glue dots or masking tape
- foam or coloured paper shapes

Preparation & instructions

1 Draw some different shapes onto cardboard and cut them out.
2 Cut the 'mouths' out with a craft knife.
3 Stick some googly eyes above the mouths.
4 Cut off the front of each small box and tape them to the back of each alien to catch the posted shapes.
5 Stick the alien shapes to the wall with glue dots or masking tape.
6 Grab some foam shapes or make your own with coloured paper.
7 Get your children to post the correct shapes through the mouths of the shape aliens.

Through the ages

AGE 1+ Explore a circle and a triangle. Tell your toddler the shape names and prompt them to post the correct shape into the matching mouth.

AGE 2+ Explore each of the four shapes together. Can your child post the correct shape into the matching mouth?

AGE 3+ Begin looking at the properties of each shape. How many sides does each one have?

AGE 4+ Look at the names of the shapes. How many sides and how many corners does each one have? Prompt your child to explore the shapes and sort them into colours and shapes.

Rhyme time...

Have you ever been to
   Shape Planet, where
   aliens roam the land?
Feed each alien the
   correct shape to see
   their tummy expand.
Have you ever been
   to Shape Planet and
   watched the aliens eat?
Go and take a look today
   and see how many you
   complete.

Planet Mobile

It can be quite expensive to buy a planet mobile, so why not make your own? Remember to use watercolour paints to explore colour mixing; they're easier to use and make this a mess-less activity.

Preparation & instructions

what you need

- pen
- round templates in various sizes, e.g. jars, bowls, plates, saucepan lids
- cardboard or paper
- scissors
- watercolour paints
- paintbrushes
- pictures of planets and the solar system
- wire coat hanger
- foil
- needle and thread

1 Draw around your circular templates on cardboard or paper and cut them out.
2 Prompt your child to colour the planets as outlined below by age.
3 Allow the painted planets to dry.
4 Meanwhile, stretch the wire hanger into a circle and remove the hook.
5 Cover the wire circle in foil.
6 Use the needle and thread to attach the planets to the wire.
7 Add a long loop of thread to the mobile and hang it up.

Through the ages

AGE 3 MONTHS+ Your baby will be too young to appreciate any planets you make, though it can be super-therapeutic for you! What the baby will really love is to explore a foil space blanket (available online) and enjoy the rustling noise and texture. Put on some space music and away you go!

AGE 1+ Explore using watercolours with your toddler. Give them one planet at a time and supply only the colours they need for that planet; this will result in a brilliant array of planets.

AGE 2+ Show your child some pictures of planets and ask them what colours they would need for each planet.

AGE 3+ Try adding just some water to each of the cardboard circles, then gently add the different colours. You can watch the colours disperse in the water, which creates a beautiful rippled effect.

AGE 4+ Show your child a picture of the solar system, then prompt them to match the size of the cardboard circles to the planets in the picture. Which planet is biggest? Which is smallest? Can your child create a perfect solar system?

Nursery-rhyme time...
(To the tune of 'Incy Wincy Spider')

Climb aboard the spaceship, we're going to the moon.
Hurry, and get ready, we're going to blast off soon!
Put on your helmets, and buckle up real tight.
Here comes the countdown, lets count with all our might.10, 9...

TRANSPORT

TRANSPORTATION IS AN important part of everyday life, and children naturally become curious about it from an early age. They are always the first to notice an aeroplane in the sky or a truck driving past.

A transportation theme not only teaches children about what different vehicles are for and how they work, but can also be used to teach other important concepts, such as safety, emergency services, colours and even counting.

Vehicles make brilliant versatile toys; you can play with them in lots of different ways and add them to all kinds of set ups. The best thing about this topic is that it's all around you. Step outside the door, head to a road and see what types of transportation you can spot!

Here you will find five activities exploring lots of different types of transportation.

Shape Trucks

You can't lose with this activity. It can last a really long time, provided you keep trying to make new vehicles.

Preparation & instructions

what you need

- pencil
- coloured paper and black paper
- scissors
- glue stick
- large sheet of paper or cardboard

1 Cut some simple shapes in different sizes out of coloured paper. Stack sheets of variously coloured paper together and cut shapes out of the whole stack. This will save time and quickly give you an array of colours and shapes.

2 Draw some wheel-sized circles on black paper and cut them out.

3 Arrange the shapes to make vehicles (you can glue them down or just have fun rearranging them over and over).

Through the ages

AGE 1+ Explore some different shapes and get your toddler to stick them to a piece of paper – a little masterpiece to pop into the art folder!

AGE 2+ Focus on making one vehicle at a time. Start with a bus and look at how many windows you can add. Work with your child on the first vehicle, but let them lead on the second.

AGE 3+ Play copycat cars: show your child how to make a vehicle and ask them to copy each step you take. Does their car look like yours?

AGE 4+ Provide your child with lots of paper shapes and a selection of vehicles for them to try to copy.

AGE 5+ Provide your child with the paper shapes in an array of different sizes and ask them to create their own vehicles. Let them explore how they can use each of the shapes.

Nursery-rhyme time...

*The wheels on the bus go
  round and round,
Round and round,
Round and round.
The wheels on the bus go
  round and round
All day long.*

*The wipers on the bus go
  swish, swish, swish,
Swish, swish, swish,
Swish, swish, swish.
The wipers on the bus go
  swish, swish, swish
All day long.*

Ice Boats

Enjoy racing ice boats around indoors, outside, in the bath, on a tray or even just on the floor. Treat it as a fun experiment to enjoy.

Preparation & instructions

what you need

- 5–6 small jugs or clear bottles of water
- gel food colouring (5 or 6 different colours)
- adhesive putty
- ice-cube trays, the larger the better (those with rounded-base shapes work best)
- paper straws, cut into 8cm (3in) lengths
- pen, coloured paper and scissors
- glue

1 The night before you want to play this game, colour five or six small jugs or clear bottles of water with different colours. This is so you'll be able differentiate between your boats.
2 Press a small piece of adhesive putty into the bottom of each compartment of an ice-cube tray.
3 Push a straw into the putty, then add your variously coloured water.
4 Pop your trays in the freezer and leave overnight.
5 Draw different sized triangles on coloured paper – you want one per ice cube – and cut them out.
6 When the 'boats' have fully frozen, fold your triangles in half and stick them to the straws as sails.

Through the ages

Never allow your children to put the ice in their mouths! Ice can be a choking hazard, particularly when it is small, so always be alert and only play with the ice when it is large enough not to fit in the mouth. As it shrinks, use it only as an observation tool.

AGE 9 MONTHS+ Place some ice boats in the bath with your baby and let them watch as they bob up and down. Remove them as they become smaller.

AGE 1+ Place the ice boats in a tray and let your toddler explore their movement. What happens when you push them along? What is happening to each of the boats?

AGE 2+ Place two different-coloured ice boats in a tray of water. Explore how to make them move. What happens when there is no movement? What happens if you push them? Have fun racing your boats.

AGE 3+ Look at the size of the sails. How do they affect each of the boats? Which boat travels fastest?

AGE 4+ Experiment with the movement of the water. Are the larger sails or smaller sails better for making the boats travel further?

Once upon a time...
in the summer, a giant boat race takes place in the town called Rockington. Rockington is famous for its fast boats and their colourful sails. Every man, woman and child in Rockington competes in the boat race, and the winner is awarded a beautiful golden trophy. Whose boat will be the winner today?

Phonics Train

Cardboard and plastic bottle caps always make for a great activity! Screwtops are brilliant for developing those fine motor skills in little ones.

what you need

- pencil
- cardboard
- coloured pens
- glue gun
- plastic bottle caps, plus the screw part they fasten to
- coloured paper

Once upon a time...
there was a train and her name was Trina. Trina loved to keep her paintwork looking neat and shiny. She also had an obsession with wheels; in fact, she loved to change her wheels every single day to match her beautiful paintwork. Can you change Trina's wheels to make her happy? What colour wheels can you add? Do you notice anything else about Trina's wheels?

Preparation & instructions

1 Using the template on page 184, draw a train on a long piece of cardboard and colour it in.
2 Using a glue gun, stick the complete bottle tops onto the train where the wheels should be.
3 Depending on your child's age, add some additional learning to this activity as indicated below.

Through the ages

AGE 1+ Practise twisting and turning the bottle caps on and off, making the wheels go round and round. Each twist will be strengthening those hand muscles.

AGE 2+ Stick a circle of coloured paper to each of the bottle caps, and add a matching spot of colour inside the wheels. Prompt your child to unscrew all the caps, then to match them up again with the inside colour.

AGE 3+ Write some single letters on each of the bottle caps. Can your child make the sound of the letter on each cap?

AGE 4+ Add lower case letters to each of the bottle caps, and capital letters inside each of the wheels. Can your child match the letters together?

AGE 5+ Write a sentence using a bottle cap for each word. Jumble the caps up, then ask your child to read the words and put them in the correct order to make a sentence.

Car Wash

Imaginary play is the best kind, and it's even better when you haven't spent money on a toy that your child may lose interest in within a couple of weeks. Great for communication, creativity and problem-solving skills.

what you need

- recycling material, e.g. cardboard tubes, cardboard boxes, plastic pots, bottle caps
- coloured tape or coloured paper, for wrapping the tubes
- glue gun or PVA glue
- toy cars
- road tape (optional)

Once upon a time...
there stood a magnificent, clean and sparkly building. Its name, in huge bright lights for everyone to see, was Splash and Dash. It was the busiest place in town. Do you know why? It was the best car wash ever invented. Do you think you could make one even better?

Preparation & instructions

1 Set out the materials listed above and use them as directed in each age group below.

Through the ages

AGE 1+ Wrap four toilet roll tubes in coloured tape or paper and glue them together. Prompt your toddler to use them as parking spaces and to put a car in a tube of a specific colour. *Key vocabulary: car, drive, zoom*

AGE 2+ Using a cardboard box, make a simple car wash together. Use tubes as parking spaces. Cut some in half lengthways to make tracks to drive in and out of the box. *Key vocabulary: up, down, in, out*

AGE 3+ Grab a wider selection of recycling materials and guide your child into creating their own ideas for a car wash, e.g. 'This tube could be a tunnel'. *Key vocabulary: ramp, tunnel*

AGE 4+ Let your child take the lead. Only intercept if they are finding the concept difficult. Try and spark their imagination by finding a video of a car wash that you can watch together. *Key vocabulary: vehicles, car, truck, van*

AGE 5+ Let your child make the model, adding road tape if they wish. Support them only by using the glue gun. *Key vocabulary: roof, wheels, windscreen (windshield), bonnet (hood)*

Fire Engine Puzzle

Puzzles are brilliant for working on problem-solving skills, memory skills and hand–eye coordination. This one is both a puzzle and a messy play activity – your children will love it!

Preparation & instructions

what you need

- pencil
- cardboard
- scissors
- coloured pens
- craft knife
- glue gun
- clear sticky-back plastic (self-adhesive plastic sheet) or sticky tape
- wipe-clean red marker pen or paint
- whipped cream or shaving foam, depending on age
- sponge

1 Draw two identical rectangles, a little bigger than A4 (US letter) size, on cardboard and cut them out.
2 Using the template on page 191, draw a fire engine on one of the cardboard rectangles and colour it in.
3 Using a craft knife, cut around the fire engine, hose, ladder, extinguisher and axe and set them aside.
4 Using a glue gun, stick the rectangle with the fire engine-shaped hole to the other cardboard rectangle, and draw an outline of a fire in front of the fire engine.
5 Cover the outline in clear sticky-back plastic or sticky tape.

Through the ages

AGE 1+ Show your toddler the puzzle and lift out just the fire engine. Prompt them to put the engine back in the correct place. Squirt whipped cream onto the fire and let your child explore it in any way they want (finger, hands, mouth).

AGE 2+ Show your child the puzzle with just the fire engine and ladder in position. Lift these pieces out, then prompt your child to put them back in the correct places, together naming the different parts of the fire engine, e.g. wheel, roof, etc. Colour the fire with a wipe-clean marker or paint. Get your child to 'put out the fire' by spraying shaving foam on it, then washing it away with a sponge.

AGE 3+ Show your child the puzzle with just the fire engine, ladder and hose in position. Discuss what each thing would be used for. What does your child think causes a fire? Colour the fire with a wipe-clean marker pen or paint. Get your little one to 'put out the fire' by spraying shaving foam on it and washing it away with a sponge.

AGE 4+ Show your child the puzzle with all the parts in place, then lift them out and complete the puzzle together. Discuss what all the equipment is and what a firefighter could possibly use it for. Colour the fire with a wipe-clean marker pen or paint. Try writing numbers or letters onto the fire and get your little one to 'put out the fire' when they have told you the correct number or letter/sound.

Question time...
Talk about fire safety, firefighters and different kinds of equipment. Who drives a fire engine? What is their job? What causes fires? What tools and equipment do they need? Some fires are put out with water and other fires are put out with foam – do you know why? Do you have anything in your house to tell you if there is a fire?

UNDER THE SEA

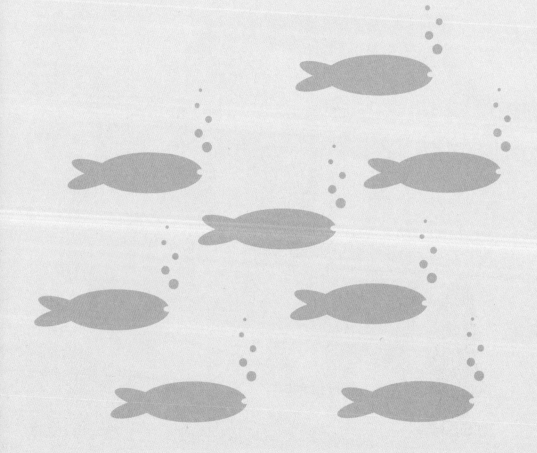

THE OCEANS TAKE up 70 per cent of the Earth's surface, so imagine the wonders you and your children can explore together when learning about what's under the sea. There are so many extraordinary and beautiful things to discover. Some of those things are so unusual that they seem almost magical. I never knew about the wonderful creatures that lived in our waters until my boys started showing an interest. I now know the difference between a sawfish and a swordfish – wonders will never cease!

Learning about the ocean does not mean that you actually have to go there. Some of it can be explored outside in a water tray, indoors on a tea tray or even in the bath. The world is your oyster (pun intended).

Here are five wonderful activities to explore sea creatures and the ocean with your children.

Polly the Petal Fish

Can your child stick petals on a cardboard fish to give it some scales? You can use anything from a nature walk and they don't all have to be the same colour.

Preparation & instructions

what you need

- petals or leaves
- coloured pens
- cardboard
- glue

1 Go on a nature hunt with your child to find petals and leaves in different colours.
2 Using the template on page 181, draw an outline of a fish on a piece of cardboard and colour it in.
3 Set out all your flowers and leaves, then let your child take the lead in deciding what colours they think will be the most beautiful.
4 Help them stick the petals or leaves to the fish's body to create some beautiful scales.

Through the ages

AGE 1+ Go on a nature hunt and explore the different colours, textures and plants. Collect the ones your toddler likes best, then get them to decorate the fish in any way that they want.

AGE 2+ Collect two colours of petals or leaves to stick on your fish. Can your child identify the two different colours? What patterns can they create?

AGE 3+ Begin to decorate your fish in clear rows; one petal or leaf after another. Concentration is key here.

AGE 4+ Start a two-part pattern, e.g. green leaf, pink petal, green leaf, pink petal. Can your child repeat the pattern?

AGE 5+ Can you come up with some more complex patterns, involving a sequence of three or more colours?

Once upon a time...
there was a fish called Polly. Polly was a small fish but she had a big heart. She was the kindest fish in the whole ocean. One day, Polly looked in the mirror and felt a little sad. More than anything in the whole world, she wanted to have brightly coloured scales. Can you be a kind friend to Polly and find her some beautiful scales?

Galaxy of Starfish

Did you know that a group of starfish is called a galaxy? In this multi-part activity, which can be enjoyed over several days, you can have fun making your very own galaxy of starfish.

Preparation & instructions

what you need

- Salt dough (see page 172)
- 2 baking sheets lined with greaseproof paper or baking parchment
- bowl of cereal loops
- star cookie cutter
- children's plastic knife, for making patterns
- tray, sand and shells (optional)

1 Preheat the oven to its lowest temperature while you prepare the salt dough, involving your child if you wish.
2 Set out your baking sheets, cereal loops and cookie cutter. (If you don't have a star-shaped cutter, you can make one out of cardboard and stick it with a glue gun.)
3 Roll out the dough to about 1.5cm (⅝ in) thick and work with your child to stamp out some stars, bending each point slightly to make realistic curves.
4 Decorate the starfish with the cereal loops. You can leave the loops in place, or use them just to make indentations. You can also make patterns using the tip of a plastic knife.
5 Place the starfish on the baking sheets and dry in the oven for 3 hours. Alternatively, leave to air-dry for 2 days.
6 When the starfish are cool and dry, you can paint them, or play with them just as they are.

Through the ages

AGE 6 MONTHS+ Help your baby to make salt dough handprints that look like starfish. Cut out a large circle of dough and press your baby's hand into it. You can let it dry and save it as a lovely keepsake.

AGE 1+ Prepare the salt dough shapes as in step 3. Prompt your toddler to push the loops into the dough using their index finger.

AGE 2+ Using the cutter, can your child stamp shapes? (You will need to remove the dough from the cutter.) Practise using the pincer grip to pick up the loops.

AGE 3+ Prompt your child to stamp out the starfish and remove the dough from the cutter. Remind them to use gentle fingers so they don't break the starfish.

AGE 4+ Prompt your child to roll out the dough themselves. Get them to stamp out the starfish, remove the dough from the cutter and decorate with the loops.

AGE 5+ Prompt your child to do all the above, then show them how to make imprints with the cereal loops. Encourage them to make patterns in other ways.

Once upon a time...
a lonely starfish sat on the glistening sand. He was hoping for a friend to be washed ashore, but although he waited all day, no one came. The lonely starfish began to cry. He closed his eyes and wished for a friend. Can you make the starfish's wish come true? How many friends can you make for him?

Help the Sea Animals

This activity is a brilliant conversation starter at any age. Your child will be instantly aware of unnatural objects in natural habitats.

Preparation & instructions

what you need

- trays or bowls
- sand and/or water (make taste-safe sand for little ones, see page 173)
- shells and stones
- plastic recyclables, e.g. packaging, bottles, bags
- sea creature or animal toys

1 Set up one or two trays with sand and/or water, then add some shells and stones.
2 'Trap' some sea creatures or animals in the packaging, e.g. a plastic bottle trapping an animal's fin.
3 Ask your child to clean up the beach and set the animals free.

Through the ages

AGE 1+ Set up a tray with taste-safe sand or water. While your toddler is playing, throw in a piece of litter. See how they react. *Key vocabulary: no, bad, bin (trash can)*

AGE 2+ Set up a tray with sand or water. While your child is playing, distract them and throw in different litter. What doesn't belong on the beach? *Key vocabulary: litter, bin (trash can), rubbish (garbage), recycle*

AGE 3+ Ask your child to free all the animals from the litter and get them to explain what harm could come to the animals. *Key vocabulary: harmful, environment, ocean, recycle*

AGE 4+ Can you begin to categorise the litter? Plastic, paper, etc. What can be recycled? *Key vocabulary: plastic, paper, cans, cardboard, recyclable*

AGE 5+ After cleaning up the beach, talk about your local environment. What places have you been to where you've seen litter? What could we do to help?

Once upon a time...
there was a beach with golden sand beside a glistening turquoise sea. Every day, people would visit the beach to enjoy its beauty. Gradually, though, its beauty began to disappear. It became a mess because people dropped litter all over the sand. Can you help to clean up the beach?

Mark the Shark

Here's a chance to combine dentistry with number work! This interactive activity provides a hands-on problem-solving experience.

Preparation & instructions

what you need

- pens or paint
- sturdy cardboard box
- scissors
- strong glue
- cocktail sticks (toothpicks)
- craft knife
- wipe-clean board or piece of cardboard covered in clear sticky tape
- wipe-clean marker pen
- children's tweezers

1 Using the template on page 185, draw a shark on a cardboard box and colour it in.
2 Cut 10 small triangles out of white cardboard.
3 Stick each triangle to a cocktail stick.
4 Make some slits in the shark's mouth so that your child can easily add and remove the teeth.
5 Write a sum on your wipe-clean board.
6 Get your child to add or remove the shark's teeth to work out the answer to the sum.

Through the ages

AGE 1+ Play and prompt your toddler to add and remove the teeth. Have a go at counting each of the teeth aloud for your little one to hear.

AGE 2+ Prompt your child to count each of the teeth. Which row of teeth has the most? Which row has the least?

AGE 3+ Simple addition through play is the best way to introduce mathematical concepts, e.g. Mark has three teeth. How many would he have if we added two more? Give your child some tweezers and ask them to add and remove the teeth as required.

AGE 4+ Play around with simple subtraction, e.g. Mark has ten teeth in total. He needs to have three teeth removed, so how many does he have left?

AGE 5+ Write a number sentence on your wipe-clean board. Watch while your child attempts to find the answer using Mark the shark.

Once upon a time...
a shark called Mark lived in the deep, dark ocean. Everyone was afraid of him because he had the sharpest teeth. One day, however, Mark cracked a tooth. Can you become a shark dentist and help to remove Mark's cracked tooth?

Let's Go Fishing

Water play is always a winner in my house, but this activity extends water play even further. Let's go fishing!

Preparation & instructions

what you need

- marker pens
- clear plastic packaging
- scissors
- paper clips
- tray
- water
- stones and/or shells (optional)
- scoop
- magnetic wands, or glue small magnets onto gift ribbon attached to bamboo skewers (see photo)
- magnetic letters and numbers

1 Draw small fish shapes on plastic packaging and cut them out.
2 Draw eyes and gills on the fish, then colour them in.
3 Add a paper clip to each of the fish.
4 Fill a tray with water and supply your child with shells and stones to create their own rockeries.
5 Provide your child with a magnetic wand or bamboo rod (pole) and go fishing.

Through the ages

AGE 1+ Can your toddler use their hands or a scoop to catch the fish?

AGE 2+ Invite your child to use a magnetic wand or rod to catch the fish.

AGE 3+ Can your child catch the red fish? The blue fish?

AGE 4+ Can your child catch five fish? Hide some magnetic letters and numbers in the tray and ask your child to find them. What words can you make from the letters? Put the numbers in the correct order.

AGE 5+ Can your child make their own magnetic fish or sea creature to pull from the ocean?

Once upon a time... on a day when the tide was low, a rock pool glimmered in the sun. Inside, there were lots of little fish who wanted to get back to the ocean because it was getting late. Can you catch them and throw them back into the sea?

WATER
AND ICE

WATER PLAY IS THE MOST open-ended sensory experience you can provide for your children, and (even better) it's the simplest kind of play there is. Just fill a tray or bath with water and give your child some bowls and spoons to provide at least half an hour well spent. It never gets boring and doesn't have to be complicated for your children to spend large amounts of time exploring.

The benefits of water play are endless, but they include fine and gross motor skills, concentration, language, mathematical skills, scientific skills... you name it! So next time you fill a tray or bowl with water, remember that list and enjoy the fact that learning through play happens naturally.

This theme is about ice as well as water, because ice is brilliantly versatile. By including it in water play you can add at least an extra half hour to any activity.

Here are five activities celebrating water and ice play.

Sensory Bags

Your child will love pushing, prodding, squeezing and tapping the content of sensory bags. Although I use laminating pouches, you don't need a laminator to make this work.

what you need

- iron or hair straighteners
- laminating pouches, size A3 or A4 (tabloid or US letter)
- water
- sensory items, e.g. water beads, pom-poms, foam shapes, plastic letters and numbers, small toys, glitter, gel food colouring, baby oil

Preparation & instructions

Depending on your child's age, you could fill the bags together.

1 Using a hot iron or hair straighteners, seal three sides of a laminating pouch. You want the seal to be about 1.5cm (½in) wide.
2 Open the bag and half-fill it with water.
3 Add any additional sensory items you like.
4 Fold over the open edge of the bag to release any trapped air, then seal with the iron or straighteners.

Through the ages

AGE 3 MONTHS+ Pop your baby on their tummy with a water sensory bag in front of them and watch them reach to touch it and explore the movement.

AGE 1+ Make a water bag and add some water beads to it. Your toddler will love moving the beads around with their hands and fingers.

AGE 2+ Make a water bag and add some pom-poms. Draw some circles on the outside and see if your child can use a finger to move a pom-pom into a circle.

AGE 3+ Make a water bag and add foam shapes, letters and numbers, pom-poms and/or small toys. Play a game of I-spy and see if your child can find the object.

AGE 4+ Slide an outline of a shape or a simple object underneath the sensory bag and see if your child can trace the lines with their finger.

Nursery-rhyme time...
I hear thunder, I hear
thunder.
Hark, don't you?
Hark, don't you?
Pitter patter raindrops,
pitter patter raindrops,
I'm wet through, so
are you.

Ice Chalk Paints

While this activity can be done indoors using a large sheet of paper, it is best done outdoors on a hard surface so that your children can make huge movements as they explore the different colour paints.

what you need

- Chalk paint or Taste-safe chalk paint, depending on age (see page 174)
- adhesive putty
- ice-cube trays
- lolly (popsicle) sticks
- large sheets of paper – a wallpaper roll is ideal (optional)
- paintbrush

Preparation & instructions

1 Make your chalk paints in several colours the night before you want to do this activity.
2 Press a little adhesive putty into the bottom of each compartment in the ice-cube trays.
3 Push a lolly stick into each piece of putty.
4 Pour the various colours of chalk paint into the tray and freeze overnight.

Through the ages

AGE 1+ Make taste-safe chalk paint and spread out a large sheet of paper. Explore with your toddler how the paints melt. Can you paint a rainbow together?

AGE 2+ Experiment with the ice cubes. Prompt your child to paint their hands and feet, and to make footprints.

AGE 3+ Encourage your child to make different marks with the ice cubes. Prompt them to use the lolly sticks, their hands and feet, and even a paintbrush. What do they notice happens when they change tools?

AGE 4+ Look at a wet painting and then look at a dry painting. What does your child notice is different between wet and dry paint?

AGE 5+ Explore mixing the chalk paint colours. Can it be done? What happens to each of the colours? Prompt your child to tell you exactly what they have painted.

Question time...

Have you ever used ice to paint with? What do you think will happen to the ice? Do you think the paint will look like usual paint? What kinds of colours do you think you could make? Do you think you could mix the colours? What will you paint today?

Foam Play

Soap foam is fluffy and smooth; one of the best textures ever. It's ideal for this sensory version of hide and seek.

what you need

- Soap foam (see page 174)
- tray or large bowl
- small plastic toys
- plastic cups and bowls

Preparation & instructions

1 Place the soap foam in a tray or bowl.
2 Add some small toys and away you go.

Through the ages

AGE 9 MONTHS+ Add some favourite bath toys to the bowl and watch your baby explore the foam.

AGE 1+ Give your toddler some cups and bowls and let them explore filling and emptying them with the foam. *Key vocabulary: more, bubble*

AGE 2+ Hide some of your child's favourite toys in the foam and ask them to squeeze the foam to find one toy at a time. Can they name the toy? What objects can they find when they splash the foam? *Key vocabulary: pour, squeeze, splash*

AGE 3+ Prompt your child to find one toy at a time and to guess what it could be before pulling it out. Ask questions as you go. Is it big or small? Is it rough or smooth? *Key vocabulary: squish, squeeze, squirt, rough, smooth, slippery*

AGE 4+ Explore using descriptive language. You go first – find a toy by feeling and describe it to your child and see if they can guess what it is. Can they do the same and make you guess? *Key vocabulary: hard, rough, textured, smooth, slippery, shiny*

Question time...

Have you ever wondered what your toys get up to when you're not there? Maybe they all jump into a giant bubble bath with the best bubbles in the world: rainbow bubbles, silky bubbles, smooth bubbles and fluffy bubbles. Come and see why I think this. When we got back today, I noticed a big splash on the floor and right next to it was this bubble tray. Shall we find out who is hiding inside?

Lost and Found

In this great time-filling activity, children have to melt or crack ice to reveal different things hiding within. They love it!

what you need

- random items, e.g. pom-poms, spoon, key, coins, etc.
- cardboard
- pen
- clear sticky-back plastic (self-adhesive plastic sheet) or sticky tape
- small glass bowl, preferably flat-bottomed
- water
- tray
- bowl of salt with plastic spoon
- plastic letters (upper and lower case)
- colour gel (optional)

Preparation & instructions

1 Place your random items on a piece of cardboard and draw around them.
2 Cover the cardboard with clear sticky-back plastic or sticky tape.
3 Pour around 2cm (¾in) water into a glass bowl, add two objects and freeze for 1 hour. Repeat this process until your container is full and all the objects are 'trapped' at different levels in the ice. (Freezing everything in one go makes the activity much harder to complete.) Try adding a different colour each time to create a rainbow effect to your ice.

Through the ages

AGE 1+ Freeze just some pom-poms in the water. Place them on the tray and watch the ice melt and release them. Have fun with the pom-pom soup you're left with.

AGE 2+ Freeze about five items in the water. Place the ice block on the tray and give your toddler some warm water to help release the objects from the ice.

AGE 3+ Freeze as many objects as you want and place the ice block on the tray. Provide your child with salt and warm water to melt the ice. Can they find the correct place for each item on the cardboard sheet?

AGE 4+ Try adding some plastic letters to the water at various stages of freezing. What sounds can your child find as the ice melts? Can they match them to their capital letter?

AGE 5+ Using the letters they find in the ice, what words can your child create? Write a list of CVC words, such as cat, dog, rat, pet, etc., and place it next to the ice tray. Can they find the letters to make the words in the list?

Once upon a time...
there was a cold, empty school all because the children were on holiday. In one classroom was a box of lost frozen things. Can you help to unfreeze them and put them where they belong?

Fill to the Line

What child doesn't love pouring, filling and emptying? This simple craft requires patience, hand–eye coordination and gross motor control, and will keep your littlest ones occupied for ages. It is best tackled outdoors, but can be done indoors on top of towels or inside a large tray.

what you need

- permanent marker or rubber bands
- plastic bottles of different sizes
- gel food colouring
- large jug of water
- small jugs and cups

Preparation & instructions

1 Draw a line or place a rubber band around each bottle at different heights.
2 Add some food colouring to the jug of water – this will make the levels in the bottles easier to see.
3 Decant some of the water into a small jug and prompt your child to fill each bottle to the line.

Through the ages

AGE 1+ Give your toddler the empty bottles and let them enjoy pouring, filling, emptying and splashing plain water.

AGE 2+ Have a tea party. Can your child fill the teacups without them overflowing? This is the first step in filling to the line.

AGE 3+ Prompt your child to fill each of the bottles to the line with the coloured water. Remind them to go slowly and to concentrate. This is all about precision.

AGE 4+ Ask your child to fill each bottle to the line. Which one has the most? Which one has the least? Which one is full or empty?

AGE 5+ Provide your child with water in three primary colours: blue, yellow and red. Mark a purple line on one bottle, a green line on another, and an orange line on a third. Can your child mix the coloured waters to match and then fill to the line?

Nursery-rhyme time...
Five green bottles
*   standing on the wall,*
Five green bottles
*   standing on the wall,*
And if one green bottle
*   should accidentally fall,*
There'd be four green
*   bottles standing on*
*   the wall.*

Recipes

Salt Dough

270g (2¼ cups) plain (all-purpose)
   flour, plus extra for dusting
270g (scant 1 cup) salt
235ml (scant 1 cup) cold water

1 Combine all the ingredients in a
   bowl and mix until a dough forms.
2 Shape the dough into a ball and
   knead it on a floured work surface
   until no longer sticky.
3 Use the dough as directed in the
   activities.

Playdough

270g (2¼ cups) plain (all-purpose) flour
200g (¾ cup) salt
2 tbsp cream of tartar
470ml (scant 2 cups) boiling water
2 tbsp vegetable oil
gel food colouring (optional)

1 Place all the dry ingredients in a
   bowl and mix together.
2 Stir in the water and oil and
   mix well.
3 Using a cocktail stick (toothpick),
   add the food colouring a drop at a
   time, mixing until you get the colour
   you want.
4 Allow the dough to cool, then
   knead until soft and smooth. If it
   sticks to your work surface or hands,
   add a little more flour.

Sand Playdough

135g (generous 1 cup) plain
   (all-purpose) flour
435g (1¼ cups) sand
200g (¾ cup) salt
2 tbsp cream of tartar
470ml (scant 2 cups) boiling water
2 tbsp vegetable oil

1 Combine all the dry ingredients in
   a bowl.
2 Mix in the wet ingredients, then set
   aside to cool.
3 Once cool, knead the dough until
   soft and smooth. If it sticks to your
   work surface or hands, add a little
   more flour.

Taste-Safe Sand (option 1)

135g (generous 1 cup) plain (all-purpose) flour
120g (4 cups) puffed rice cereal

1 Raw flour straight from the bag contains bacteria, so it must be heated before use in a taste-safe activity to ensure it is safe to consume. Place it in a bowl in the microwave and heat on High for 1½ minutes, stirring every 30 seconds. Alternatively, spread the flour on a baking sheet and place in an oven preheated to 180°C/160°C Fan/350°F/Gas mark 4 for 5 minutes. Allow to cool.
2 Once it has cooled, place the flour and rice cereal in a food processor and pulse until the mixture has the texture of sand.

Taste-Safe Sand (option 2)

This recipe makes the most realistic sand.

135g (generous 1 cup) plain (all-purpose) flour
210g (1½ cups) brown sugar
180g (1¼ cups) quinoa
200g (3 cups) coffee granules

1 Heat-treat the flour as described above (Taste-Safe Sand option 1).
2 Once it has cooled, mix the flour with all the other ingredients in a tray.

Taste-Safe Mud

270g (2¼ cups) plain (all-purpose) flour
4 tbsp cocoa powder
235-470ml (about 1–2 cups) water

1 Heat-treat the flour as described (see Taste-Safe Sand, option 1).
2 Combine the heat-treated flour and cocoa powder in a bowl.
3 Stir in the water a bit at a time until you have your desired consistency. I like to make it quite wet so that it looks like a muddy puddle, but you can make it thicker if you prefer by adding less water.

Chia Seed Slime

85g (½ cup) chia seeds
470ml (scant 2 cups) water
gel food colouring (optional)
240g (scant 2 cups) cornflour (cornstarch)

1 Place the chia seeds and water in a bowl.
2 Add a few drops of food colouring (if using) and stir well.
3 Cover with clingfilm (plastic wrap) and refrigerate overnight.
4 The next day, add the cornflour a bit at a time, stirring it in with a fork until you have a thick slime. This can keep its shape when held, but returns to liquid form when released.

Play Snow

235ml (scant 1 cup) hair conditioner
650g (5 cups) bicarbonate of soda
(baking soda)

1 Pour the hair conditioner into a tray.
2 Add the bicarbonate about a
quarter at a time and stir with a fork
until you have a crumbly, pliable
'snow'.
3 The snow can be used immediately
after it's made, but try refrigerating
it for an hour or so to make it feel
cold, like real snow!

Taste-Safe Play Snow

945g (scant 8 cups) plain (all-purpose)
flour
220ml (generous 1 cup) coconut oil

1 Heat-treat the flour as described on
page 173 (Taste-Safe Sand,
option 1).
2 Once the flour has cooled, place it
in a bowl.
3 Gradually add the oil, mixing with a
spoon or your hands.
4 This snow can be used immediately
after it's made, but try refrigerating
it for an hour or so to make it feel
cold, like real snow!

Cloud Dough

945g (scant 8 cups) plain (all-purpose)
flour
235ml (scant 1 cup) baby oil

1 Place the flour in a bowl.
2 Gradually add the oil, mixing with a
spoon or your hands.
3 Place in a tray and use as required.

Chalk Paint

coloured chalks
1 tbsp water per colour

1 Place a coloured chalk stick in a
sealable plastic bag (one colour
per bag).
2 Using a rolling pin or hammer, crush
the chalk into a fine powder.
3 Add the water and stir until a paste
forms.

Taste-Safe 'Chalk' Paint

1 tbsp cornflour (cornstarch)
2 tbsp water
gel food colouring

1 Place the cornflour, water and a
drop of food colouring in a bowl
and mix well.
2 Continue mixing in the colouring
a drop at a time until you get the
shade you want.
3 Repeat this process to make as
many colours as you like.

Soap Foam

240ml (scant 1 cup) water
3 tbsp washing-up liquid (dish soap) or
baby bubble bath

1 Put all the ingredients into a food
processer and whizz until firm
and fluffy.
2 Alternatively, put the ingredients
in a bowl and whizz with a stick
blender until firm and fluffy.

Rainbow Dried Rice, Pasta or Chickpeas

500g (1lb 2oz) dried rice, pasta or chickpeas

gel food colouring, if making this taste-safe for very small children

poster paint, if making this for older children

1 Place your dried ingredient in sealable plastic bags, 1 bag per colour.
2 Add a small amount of food colouring or paint to each bag, seal tightly and rub it in.
3 Empty the contents of each bag into its own parchment-lined baking tray and leave to dry overnight.

Rainbow Cooked Spaghetti

1 handful dried spaghetti
gel food colouring

1 Cook the spaghetti in a pan of boiling water until al dente (if it's too soft it will fall apart). Drain well.
2 Decide how many colours you want to make, then put a handful of spaghetti, per colour, into the same number of sealable plastic bags.
3 Add a small amount of food colouring to each bag, seal tightly and rub it into the spaghetti.
4 Leave in the bag for 5 minutes.
5 Place the spaghetti, one colour at a time, in a colander and rinse with water. This stops the colour transferring to your hands when you come to use it. Transfer to separate bowls.

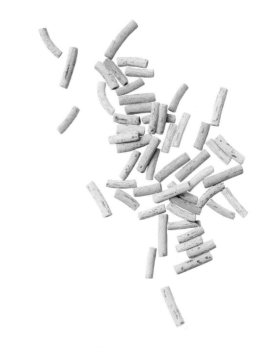

Shortbread

125g (1 stick + 1 tbsp) softened butter

60g (¼ cup) caster sugar (superfine sugar)

1 tsp vanilla extract

200g (1¼ cups) plain (all-purpose) flour, plus extra for dusting

1 Cream the butter, sugar and vanilla together in a bowl.
2 Mix in the flour until a smooth dough forms.
3 Turn the dough onto a floured work surface and roll out until about 1cm (½in) thick.
4 Using cookie cutters, stamp out shapes and place them on a baking sheet.
5 Chill in the fridge for 30 minutes.
6 Preheat the oven to 180°C/160°C Fan/350°F/Gas mark 4.
7 Bake the shortbread for 15–20 minutes, until golden.

Resources

Lots of activities in this book feature the use of recyclables, so are effectively free. The other items listed below are useful but not essential. Please feel free to adapt any of the activities with things you can find around your own home.

Recyclables to save

Bubble wrap

Cardboard

Cardboard tubes (from toilet rolls, etc.)

Egg boxes

Glass jars

Lolly sticks (popsicle sticks)

Plastic bottle caps, plus the screw part they fasten to

Plastic packaging, such as fruit punnets

Straws

Tin cans

Yoghurt pots

Top tip: Cut up your cardboard boxes as you get them so that they're easier to store.

Craft essentials

Children's scissors

Craft knife (adult use only)

Craft sticks

Clothes pegs (clothes pins)

Cocktail sticks (toothpicks)

Cotton wool (cotton balls)

Dot stickers

Gel food colouring

Glue gun (adult use only)

Googly eyes

PVA glue

Paint sticks, crayons, paints, felt-tips (My favourite drawing tools for young children are paint sticks because they are easy to use and the colours are extremely vibrant.)

Pom-poms

Paper, white and coloured

Sticky-back plastic (self-adhesive plastic sheet) and/or sticky tape (clear)

Wipe-clean marker pens

Open-ended toys

Animals

Bugs

Building blocks

Cars

Dinosaurs

Imaginative play sets, e.g. doctor's kit, tea set

Instruments

Magnetic tiles

Sea creatures

Trains

Learning resources

Children's tongs

Children's tweezers

Coloured counters

Dice

Foam letters and numbers

Large multifunction tray (see below right)

Magnetic numbers and letters

Magnets or magnetic tape

Magnifying glasses

Pipettes

Threading beads

Household objects

Baking trays

Clothes pegs (clothes pins)

Jugs

Plastic cups, bowls and plates

Spoons

Tongs

Trays (dipping trays, breakfast trays)

Under-the-bed storage boxes

Store-cupboard ingredients

Bicarbonate of soda (baking soda)

Black beans

Cornflour (cornstarch)

Flour (plain/all-purpose)

Gel food colouring

Hair conditioner

Oil (any type)

Pasta

Rice

Salt

Vinegar

Washing-up liquid (dish soap)

Further information

Sensory table (Flisat) –
www.ikea.com

Mud kitchen –
www.mudkitchens.co.uk

Multifunction tray (PlayTRAY) –
www.inspiremyplaystore.com

Activities by type

Super-Speedy Ideas

Copycat Bugs
Rubber Band Guitar
Drum Set
Emotion Stones
Weather Wheel
Shape Trucks
Fill to the Line

Nature & Outdoor Play

Nature Scavenger Hunt
Shape Finders
Nature Bunnies
Leaf Monsters
Polly the Petal Fish

Quiet Time

Harold the Hedgehog
Sun Catcher Butterfly
Tweeze the Spots
X-Ray Craft
Blossom Tree
Planet Mobile

Sensory Play

Shirley the Sheep
Sponge Footprints
Dino Slime
Puffy Paints
Rainbow Rice
Snowmen
Intergalactic Fizzers
Ice Chalk Paints

Baby Play

Spaghetti Worms
Dinosaur Sensory Bottles
Rain Stick Bottle

Sensory Bags
Foam Play

Perfect for Sibling Play

Glass Jar Xylophone
Billy's Body
Healthy-Eating Harry
Brush your Teeth
Tambourine
Eat the Rainbow
Conker Run
Ice Boats
Help the Sea Animals
Let's Go Fishing
Lost and Found

Phonics Play

Mrs Crabby Claws
Posting Machine
Play Beach
Moonscapes
Phonics Train

Maths Play

Pegasaurus
Adding Machine
Shape Aliens
Bug Count
Mark the Shark

Projects to do over a number of days

Animal Fossils
Excavation
Dino Eggs
Sunflower Craft
Space Cookies
Car Wash
Fire Engine Puzzle
Galaxy of Starfish

LITTLE HAPPY LEARNERS

Templates

Here are a selection of templates that can be traced or photocopied when an activity requires some drawing to be done. Some templates need to be enlarged when photocopied, such as Healthy-Eating Harry. Of course, you can draw free-hand if you prefer – your children will always be impressed by what you produce!

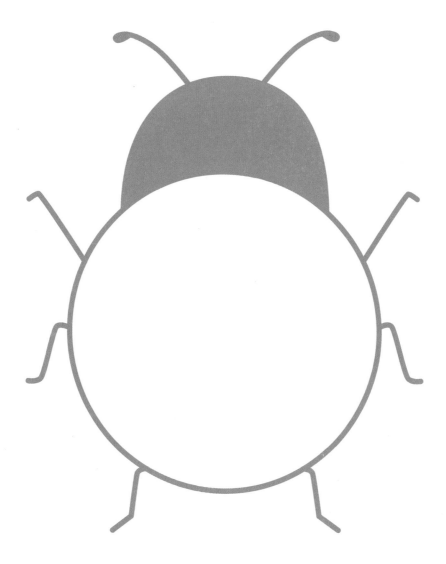

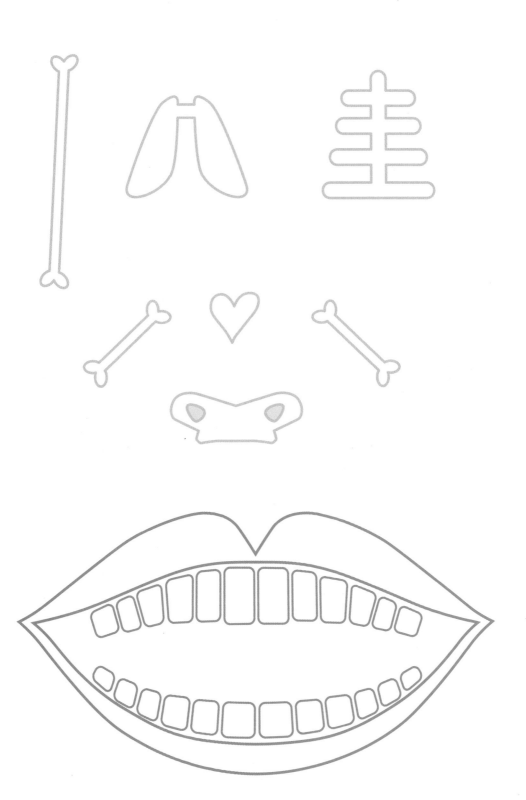

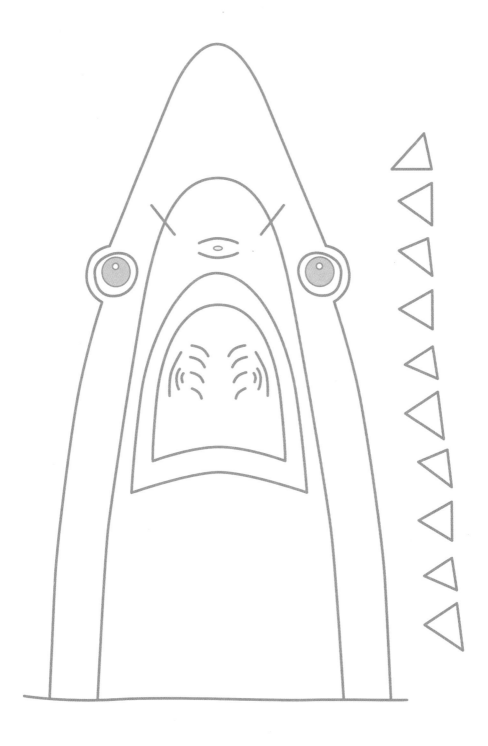

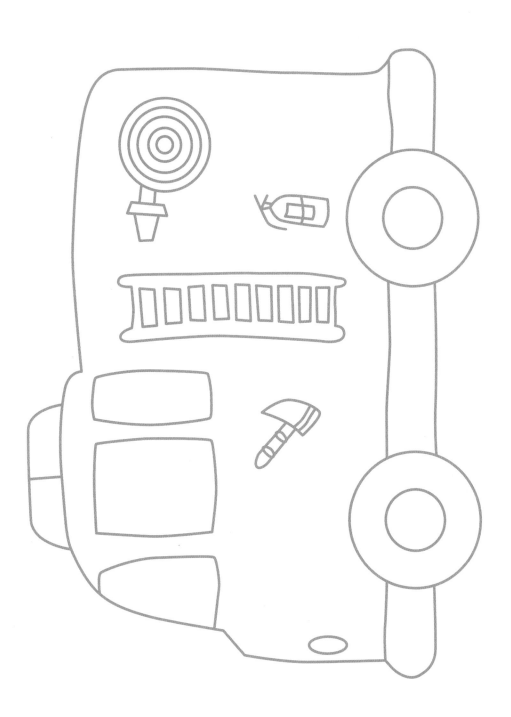

Acknowledgements

Thank you to:

Ted, you made me a mummy and taught me to take life slower. Finn, you have taught me to love harder and show a little more patience. Edie you have taught me to never take a moment for granted and to enjoy every single smile. The three of you have made me a much better version of myself, I will always try my hardest, I might not always get it right but thank you for loving me anyway.

Adam, you have always been my biggest cheerleader, every single day for the last 10 years. You have helped me to believe in myself and you support our family like no other. You put up with my tantrums and the constant sound of dry shampoo. I will always be grateful for you. I love you.

Mum and Dad, thank you for showing me what unconditional love is. You have taught me to always strive for greatness but, above all, to put my family first, just like you have always done. I will forever be grateful for your love, our family and the home you made for us (and the crumpets).

Rachel, Becky, Charlie and Chloe, my sisters, my best friends. I continue to learn from you all, each and every day. I've watched you all become the most incredible mothers to my beautiful nieces and nephews and couldn't thank you more for the love you give to Ted, Finn and Edie. I hope this thank you makes up for all the times I stole your clothes growing up. I love you all.

To everyone at Hodder for making this happen; a special thank you to Nicky and Liv for believing in this idea right from the very start. To Isobel and Jen for making each page look more beautiful than I could have imagined and to Trish for being the best copyeditor around. I'm in awe of you all!

To Darryl, for being the first person to believe in me, probably more than myself. I cannot thank you enough.

Finally, I'd like to thank all of those who have followed our journey over on Little Happy Learners Instagram. Without you all, I would never have fulfilled this complete dream. I am eternally grateful.   Soph x

First published in Great Britain in 2022 by Yellow Kite
An imprint of Hodder & Stoughton
An Hachette UK company

1

Copyright © Sophie David 2022

Photography by Jen Rich © Hodder and Stoughton 2022

Additional photography copyright on pages 6, 9, 11, 16, 23, 25 and 27 © Chloe Hook of Life Of Soul Photography 2021

The right of Sophie David to be identified as the Author of the Work has been asserted by her in accordance with the Copyright, Designs and Patents Act 1988.

A CIP catalogue record for this title is available from the British Library

Hardback ISBN 978 1 529 39464 1
eBook ISBN 978 1 529 39465 8

Editorial Director: Nicky Ross
Assistant Editor: Olivia Nightingall
Design: Isobel Gillan
Photography: Jen Rich
Copyeditor: Trish Burgess
Production Controller: Rachel Southey

Colour origination by Altaimage London Ltd
Printed and bound in Germany by Mohn Media

Hodder & Stoughton policy is to use papers that are natural, renewable and recyclable products and made from wood grown in sustainable forests. The logging and manufacturing processes are expected to conform to the environmental regulations of the country of origin.

Yellow Kite
Hodder & Stoughton Ltd
Carmelite House
50 Victoria Embankment
London
EC4Y 0DZ

www.yellowkitebooks.co.uk
www.hodder.co.uk